Haunted Places of Cornwall

On the Trail of the Paranormal

Sheila Bird

COUNTRYSIDE BOOKS
NEWBURY BERKSHIRE

COUNTRYSIDE BOOKS
3 Catherine Road
Newbury, Berkshire

To view our complete range of books,
please visit us at
www.countrysidebooks.co.uk

ISBN 1 85306 987 6
EAN 978185306 987 1

Photographs by the author
unless otherwise stated

Designed by Peter Davies, Nautilus Design
Produced through MRM Associates Ltd., Reading
Typeset by Jean Cussons Typesetting, Diss, Norfolk
Printed by Borcombe Printers plc, Romsey

•Contents•

HAUNTED PLACES OF CORNWALL

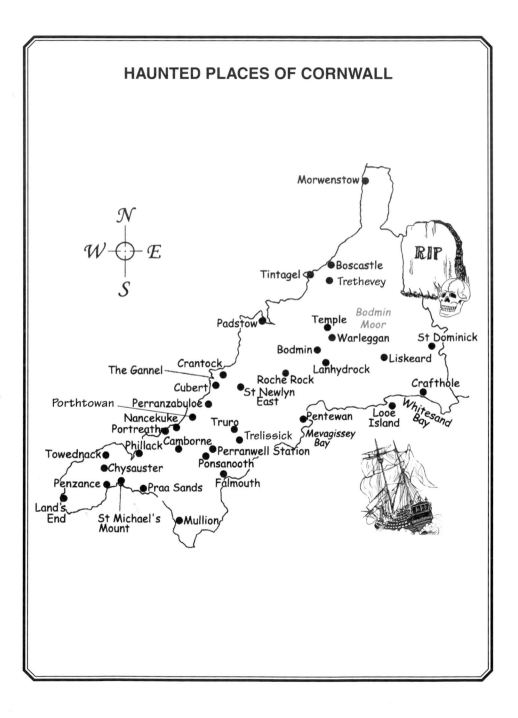

·Introduction·

From ghoulies and ghosties
And long leggity beasties
And things that go bump in the night,
Good Lord, deliver us.

(A Cornish litany)

Cornwall, with its wild moors and dramatic coastline, has been cited by experienced investigators of the paranormal as being the most haunted county in Britain. A distinctive culture evolved within this mystical landscape which had a strong supernatural element, with a widespread belief in giants, piskies, fairies, a host of other sprites, and the magical powers of white and black witches for good or ill. Phantom ships and spectral black dogs on harbour-sides would forewarn of danger at sea, while sprites known as 'buccas' or 'knockers' were thought to inhabit the mines. It paid to keep on the right side of these seen and unseen spirit presences.

The county has had a profusion of ghost-laying clergymen, including Parson Dodge of Talland, Parson Jago of Wendron and Parson Richards of Camborne. A century ago it was stated in a Cornish publication:

'There seems a greater effort at the present day to raise ghosts than to lay them; but if what we are told is true, that spirits can attach themselves inconveniently and alarmingly to those who have got in touch with them, the services of the old-fashioned ghost-layer may once more be called into request.'

Although there may be a tendency to associate ghostly stories with the dim and fanciful past, researching this book has revealed to me a current preoccupation with 'things that go bump in the night', and there is a growing interest in sophisticated hi-tech equipment, crystal pendants, divining rods and enthusiastic attendances at 'ghost night' sessions held at paranormal hotspots.

In compiling this book, I have interpreted paranormal happenings in the context of their historical background. While some traditional stories have been included, the emphasis is on little known and previously undocumented events.

Sheila Bird

BODMIN

'The county gaol, built very lately, stands in a healthy spot just outside the town. This building is laid out nearly on the plan recommended by Mr Howard, and struck us as a model for all places of confinement …'
(*Observations of the Western Counties of England: 1794–96: W.G. Maton*)

The ancient town of Bodmin, with its profusion of religious foundations also possessed a hospital for lepers and a prison for offenders from early times. It was a prestigious breakthrough in the late 18th century when a decision was made to replace the notorious County Gaol in Launceston Castle, with a purpose-built one in the more centrally located town of Bodmin, where the Assizes and Quarter Sessions were also held. It was completed in 1779 under the auspices of Sir John Call, JP, and housed a carefully planned, self-sufficient community, with prisoners working in the laundry, kitchens and prison garden. The inmates were kept busy carding and spinning wool, weaving, making mats or sawing wood. Those who got into trouble might find themselves sentenced to a hard stint on the dreaded treadmill, or a flogging, and there was a strict code of silence. Crimes such as highway robbery, burglary, sheep stealing, forgery and arson had carried the death penalty, but in Robert Peel's time, capital offences were greatly reduced and those

A view of the naval prison from the main building, where supernatural activities have occurred.
(*Simon T. Wheten, Bodmin Gaol*)

executed here after 1835 were generally murderers.

Conditions for prisoners improved in 1860, when a new prison was built, using local granite quarried by inmates. The building was noted for its fine craftsmanship and rather grim grandeur. The improved facilities included bigger cells, a hospital block, workrooms and exercise yards. The Debtors Act of 1869 brought an end to debtors being cast into gaol, and this led to a section of the prison being taken over by the Admiralty, to deal with offenders previously detained at Devonport Gaol.

Executions had traditionally been carried out at St Lawrence, but after the County Asylum was constructed on that site in 1816, public hangings took place just outside the main south wall of the prison, allowing crowds of spectators on the hillside opposite to obtain a good view of the chilling and dramatic proceedings.

A profusion of orbs, thought to represent ghostly presences in a cell at Bodmin Gaol. (Simon T. Wheten, Bodmin Gaol)

Although the grisly spectacle was intended to serve as a salutary lesson, public hangings came to be regarded as thrilling entertainment by the masses. On these occasions eager crowds converged on Bodmin with local traders exploiting the situation to the full. After the hangings the prisoners' bodies remained suspended for an hour and a minute before being taken down and buried in the prison grounds. Fragments of rope used in hangings were much in demand for their therapeutic properties, while healing powers were associated with being able to touch the corpse.

The first reaction of many of today's visitors to Bodmin Gaol is one of shock; the building is now a museum, with a restaurant, bar area and gift shop, but highlights the horrifying reality of incarceration in a more brutal age, where the doom-laden atmosphere of the stairways, corridors and cells exude the feelings of misery and despair they once encompassed. Some speak of fleeting shadowy figures, the menacing sound of heavy footsteps, and rattling and clinking noises reminiscent of the treadmill and gaolers' keys. Sensitive souls have been moved to tears after hearing screams of anguish and several people with psychic tendencies have spoken of a ghostly, angry young man with dark curly hair, in a yellowish waistcoat, who sits under a window in the naval prison, or paces up and down, and beats on the wall with knuckles clenched white, as if he wants the world to hear him.

On one recent occasion a deeply religious grandmother who came upon two girls crying on the landing near an (unmarked) condemned cell, went to comfort them and got a shock when they disappeared into thin air. They briefly reappeared as she fell to her knees and prayed for their souls. It later transpired that these child spirits are well-known to some of the mediums who make regular visits to the prison.

Spooky things have happened in the present bar area. The barman went to serve a gentleman he had seen entering and who was wearing a greatcoat and flat cap, only for him to unaccountably disappear. Candle lanterns in that bar are apt to start swinging for no apparent reason and they leap spontaneously into the air from one particular table, before smashing onto the floor.

There was some rather more benign supernatural activity hereabouts in the 17th century when young Anne Jefferies of St Teath, who possessed remarkable powers of clairvoyance and healing and claimed to commune with the fairies, was cast into Bodmin Gaol, accused of witchcraft. Despite being deprived of food and ill-treated in dank and dark conditions, she amazed everyone by emerging from her incarceration looking radiant, healthy and happy. She explained that she had been looked after by her fairy friends. However, she refused to divulge details of her relationship with these helpful little spirits, and took her secrets with her to the grave.

BODMIN MOOR

The bleak and rugged landscape of Bodmin Moor, where storm winds howl across the wild terrain, rain lashes horizontally and sudden mists descend to envelope all in an eerie, woolly silence, has always been a place of mystery and legend. Our primeval ancestors have left enduring imprints on the granite moors, which have seen marching armies and witnessed human conflict over the centuries. Some associate these with reports of phantom black figures and rider-less horses galloping across the moors and suddenly evaporating into thin air.

In bygone days the isolated moorlanders had a strong belief in little sprites (spirits). The dark and brooding Dozmary Pool was thought to be the resort of evil spirits, including the notorious John Tregeagle, who might be heard howling across the moors on wintry nights, pursued by the devil and his hounds from hell. A guidebook of 1865 recalls a conversation with two moormen at Jamaica Inn, made infamous by Daphne du Maurier. One related how he was startled by the noise of a ghostly coach and the cracking of whips while cutting peat near the pool after dark. He declared that he 'definitely heard the coach plunge under water'. The other described seeing a strange light on the solitary shore 'like a fire in a furze bush'.

*   *   *

If all this sounds a bit far-fetched, strange happenings have been reported at one of the man-made lakes in recent years. People crossing the bridge at Siblyback Reservoir, where fishing is permitted, got a surprise when the approaching figure of a man with head bent, whom they took to be a fisherman, suddenly vanished. At various times, dog-owners have reported that their pets behave nervously at the same spot, and refuse to cross the bridge.

The Charlotte Dymond memorial stone at Roughtor Ford.

*   *   *

A more easily identifiable ghostly manifestation by a watercourse occurs in the vicinity of Roughtor Ford, where a grim granite monument, erected by public subscription in Victorian times, recalls servant girl Charlotte Dymond, who was murdered there on Sunday, 14th April 1844.

The comely young woman had been in service at Penhale Farm on the northern fringes of Bodmin Moor since the age of ten. She dressed stylishly and was a bit of a coquette.

For some time, she had been in a comfortable steady relationship with farm labourer Matthew Weekes. Then one of Matthew's old adversaries came on the scene and threatened to steal Charlotte from him. On one occasion, as she set off in her Sunday best for a secret assignation with this rival, Matthew followed her and they walked together up the muddy lane and along the moorland track. He rebuked her for 'behaving disgracefully' with another man. But when Charlotte haughtily turned her back on him, declaring that she would do as she liked and wanted nothing more to do with him, he drew out his pocket-knife and lunged towards her. Fortunately, he came to his senses in time and put the knife away, but when she repeated those fateful words, he lost control. She toppled backwards, blood cascading from a ragged wound in her neck, crying 'Lord have mercy on me!' She landed at the edge of the stream and Matthew hid her outer garments and accessories in the undergrowth and flung the knife away, before returning to Penhale Farm.

Matthew Weekes was tried and found guilty of the murder of Charlotte Dymond. Just before he was executed at Bodmin Gaol, he wrote, 'See what a wretched end I have come to by loving too true'.

Since that time, and especially on the anniversary of her death, Charlotte has been seen walking in the area, clad in a gown, a red shawl and a silk bonnet. Sentries from the Old Volunteers swore that they had seen her ghostly figure walking nightly across the moor to the spot where she had been murdered and were reluctant to stand guard. Servicemen from the Second World War also had similar stories to relate.

Some years ago a man who had been fishing in moorland streams, and relishing the solitude, was returning to an inn where he was staying, when he was surprised to see a young woman in a full-length green striped dress, with red shawl and silk bonnet, walking through the marshes at the foot of Roughtor. She paused every now and again to look around as if searching for someone, shading her eyes with her hand as she did so. He called out 'Goodnight', but received no reply. When he reached the inn, the landlord told him that he must have seen the ghost of poor Charlotte Dymond, as many others had done. Her story has been immortalised in *The Ballad of Charlotte Dymond*, by Cornish poet Charles Causley.

*   *   *

A phantom rider on horseback seen in the courtyard of Jamaica Inn recalls the days when stagecoaches called here and travellers lived in fear of highwaymen on the bleak and lonely moors. The isolated hostelry on the old carriers' track between Bodmin and Launceston became a coaching inn after the coming of the turnpike road in 1769. As keen winds rattle the portals of this evocative, slate-hung building, with its shuttered leaded light windows, today's travellers might sense some shadowy figures seemingly going about their dubious activities of days of yore.

There have long been tales of haunted happenings here. One of the best known concerns the mysterious traveller, who called for a drink one night, and left his pot of ale on the bar counter as he was summoned outside by some unseen stranger. He never returned and his lifeless body was discovered the following morning on moorland nearby. Various landlords have attributed the sound of ghostly footsteps along the passageway to the bar to his spirit returning to finish off the drink he left behind. Sightings of a phantom figure sitting on the wall outside have also been associated with this murder.

Jamaica Inn has recently become the focus of paranormal investigations, with several spooky manifestations being recorded. A female phantom apparently walks straight through tables in the bar, and several diners have had a surprise when the tall, broad figure of a man pacing backwards and forwards in the restaurant disappeared before their very eyes. Mention has also been made of a dark burly ghost who suddenly makes a dash from the Stable Bar towards the courtyard, as if rushing to meet a coach newly arrived.

One of the bedrooms is said to be haunted by a man in a three-cornered hat and long, waisted greatcoat, who wafts past the end of the bed and disappears through a large wardrobe. The room becomes very cold when he is about to put in an appearance.

Staff occupying quarters in an adjacent building have spoken of a monk-like figure in a hood and long cape, which seemed to be very real as it progressed from the kitchen to the bedroom, looking downwards with head bent slightly forwards. Strange things have also been reported in the mundane environment of the boiler room. Long ago, when it was a small farmstead this area was thought to have been the place where animals were slaughtered. Lights switch themselves on and off in the cold and spooky atmosphere, and staff prefer not to go there alone.

*   *   *

The old route across the moors ran through the little hamlet of Temple, which derived its name from the Knights Templar, a military and religious order established in the 12th century, with a network across Europe. After its church fell into disrepair in the 18th century, Temple became a remote and rarely visited part of the diocese of Exeter, and irregularities began to creep in. The place achieved a certain notoriety on account of its unconventional approach

Templar.

Could the eerie presence at Temple be associated with the 12th-century Knights Templar?

Temple church in ruins, before being rebuilt in 1883.

to villains, rebels and other outcasts of society. The marrying of couples without banns or licence led to a reputation of being the 'Gretna Green of Bodmin Moor', while the sheltering of unmarried mothers gave rise to the wry expression, 'Send her to Temple Moors'.

The diocese put a stop to all this, and the church which had fallen again into a state of neglect, was rebuilt and rededicated in 1883.

Along with the broadcaster Duncan Warren, I had a spooky experience inside this little church while recording a programme for Radio Cornwall. As I was recounting some of the strange events of the past into his hand-held microphone, he suddenly looked alarmed, his hand began to shake and his voice developed a tremor, which the listeners noticed when the programme went out on air. As we left the church Duncan explained that he had been shocked by a presence just above my right shoulder, making it plain that it did not like what we were doing. He said, 'It was as though we were intruding on its territory; that we shouldn't be there'. Many years later he recalled, 'The biggest thing I will always remember is that it was just *so* cold. I said to you when we came out, "I have never felt like that before". I was absolutely *icy cold*, and yet it was a warm summer's day, if you remember.'

*   *   *

Strange things also happen in the isolated village of Warleggan, a few miles to the south of Temple, where the Rev. Frederick William Densham was vicar between 1931 and 1953. When nobody turned up to his services, this unfortunate man of the cloth, who was out of tune with his parishioners, preached to cardboard figures in the church. The situation was poignantly summed up when he recorded in his service book: 'No fog, no wind, no rain, no congregation.' He became more and more eccentric and retreated into a world of his own at the rectory, behind a high wire fence, and guarded by Alsatian dogs. He met his death on the stairs, having been unable to reach the bell push to alert his servant, who lived in the stables.

The ghostly, sad figure of the former vicar is now said to haunt the rectory (converted into flats). He wanders dolefully around the garden and along the pathway to the locked door of the charming old church in the moonlight, perhaps looking to see if he at last has a congregation.

BOSCASTLE

'Strange, striking, and utterly unique is the first aspect of this village by the sea. The gorge or valley lies between two vast precipitous hills that yawn asunder as though they had been cleft by the spells of some giant warlock of the west ...'
(*Ride from Bude to Bos*: 1870, the Rev. R. S. Hawker)

The creation of the old port of Boscastle, in a deep combe at the head of a creek on the inhospitable northern coast of Cornwall, might be regarded as a triumph of man over nature, but for the fact that the place became the focus of worldwide attention in August 2004, when a devastating flood swept through the village. Buildings and cars were swept away, but miraculously no lives were lost, thanks to heroic helicopter pilots and others. One can only wonder what the resident ghosts of Boscastle made of it all.

One of the buildings badly damaged at that time was the Museum of Witchcraft, housing some weird and wonderful exhibits, including devil dolls and ritual objects once owned by a magician. Happily this and other businesses

The door to the Museum of Witchcraft in Boscastle. (Graham King)

were up and running again the following year. Meanwhile, a blowhole in the narrow neck of land at Penally Head, known as the Devil's Bellows, continued to startle folk with its rumbustious roars and the propulsion of spectacular jets of spray across the harbour entrance.

Penally House, situated amongst trees on rising land above the harbour at the eastern side of Boscastle, is reputedly haunted. It was constructed by wealthy merchant William Sloggatt, on the site of a much earlier dwelling. He was thought to have concealed contraband goods there and various owners have spoken of the sound of footsteps inside and outside the house, while a phantom figure gliding past the window has been associated with the smuggling fraternity.

*   *   *

Unexplained happenings have also occurred just down the road at the Old Manor House, where a child was said to have been murdered. Ghostly pranks include taps being turned on. When the present owner, who is also landlord of the Napoleon Inn, has been busy baking, he has heard the sound of laughter echoing from the empty hallway. On one occasion the mixer was inexplicably turned off to a point 'beyond the click mark'. He discovered that the previous occupants of the house had also experienced disconcerting poltergeist activity with objects being thrown around in the bedroom he occupies quite happily.

*   *   *

The 16th-century Napoleon Inn, in its elevated situation in the High Street, has long enjoyed a ghostly reputation. It acquired its present name on account of a former landlord who served in Wellington's army being nicknamed

'Napoleon's man' by some wag on his return. The establishment was thought to have been used as a recruiting office and one of the resident ghosts who walks through the wall where there was formerly a door has the appearance of a foot soldier from the time of the Napoleonic Wars. Paranormal investigators have spoken of bad vibes in one of the upstairs rooms, and of a presence who may have been unhappily confined here at some time. By contrast, a rather more contented phantom, who may have been a smuggler, has been seen sitting in a corner of the bottom bar smoking a pipe.

The Napoleon Inn in the High Street at Boscastle.

*   *   *

The resident spooks of the nearby Wellington Hotel must have felt more secure than the living on that fateful day in August 2004 when, shortly after customers had been evacuated from the public rooms, a massive surge of water came rushing through the building, and continued to do so for the next 38 hours. This fine old hotel, originally known as the Boscastle Hotel, acquired its patriotic name at the time of Wellington's death in 1852. It was substantially rebuilt the following year, when the stylish turrets were added, ready to welcome the well-heeled tourists to Boscastle when it became a popular destination in the latter part of the century. Things really gained momentum after the arrival of the railway at nearby Camelford in 1893, when the trains were met by horse buses.

Unexplained thumps, bumps, bangs and scraping sounds like furniture being moved around are a regular feature of life in various parts of the hotel, but particularly in the vicinity of the dining room. Indeterminate dark shapes have been seen wafting down the stairs in the cellar after nightfall. The ghostly little boy seen in the corridor by the cellar is said to have perished whilst attempting to save another child from drowning in the ancient culvert running beneath·

the building. A girl in a cloak has been seen emerging from a solid wall and exiting through a closed window. It is thought she had thrown herself from the top of the tower after being jilted by her lover. Following alterations when the window was replaced by a door, she continued to make her departure through the closed door.

A horse bus leaves the much haunted Wellington Hotel in 1913. (Truro Museum)

Former owner Victor Tobutt got a surprise one day while working at the reception desk, when he saw a substantial man in a frock coat, frilled shirt, boots and leather gaiters in the style of an 18th-century coachman, proceed across the room and disappear through the wall. It transpired that the spectre had previously been spotted in various parts of the hotel on a number of occasions but nobody knows who he is, or rather was.

Hotel staff have been aware of an eerie presence in several of the bedrooms, while a ghostly woman, who was probably a former guest, seems to favour rooms 9 and 10. She is wont to waft through the walls and closed doors, and sometimes sits on the bed in room 10.

Room 21 also has an eerie reputation, with chambermaids reporting strange sounds. In 2003 a national ghost expert, who considers Cornwall to be 'one of the spookiest places in Britain', said that he got the fright of his life in room 21 when on two occasions his bed started moving about and he became trapped after the old-fashioned lock on the door unaccountably activated itself.

CRANTOCK AND THE GANNEL

The coastal area around Crantock has a strange and colourful past. According to legend, this was the site of the affluent city of Langarrow, whose inhabitants became idle and dissolute. The city was overwhelmed by sea and sand in a sudden tempest as an act of Divine Retribution.

The sands still hold their secrets, but it was traditionally believed that the souls of those who have lost their lives over the centuries, in the fast-flowing waters of the Gannel, inhabit the bodies of sea birds, which are so prolific in the area.

The Gannel was thought to be haunted by the spirits of those who had drowned here.

The Gannel was recognised as a port with a good share of coastal trade as early as the 13th century. The coastline proved ideal for smuggling, with contraband goods being concealed in nearby farms and cottages, as well as the Albion Inn and even the belfry of the local church. But this was also notorious shipwreck territory, with many vessels being swept on shore during the relentless Atlantic storms.

Many years ago a worried Crantock woman whose husband's ship was long overdue could not cope with the uncertainty of not knowing whether he was alive or dead. She went down to the shore with two friends and called out to him in her distress. All three of them claimed to have heard his spirit reply.

As the Gannel estuary silted up, it became increasingly hazardous to cross the primitive footbridge which was put in place to allow passage at low tide, and this has been the scene of many disasters. Some who had attempted to cross the river bed, particularly at night, when it was easy to misjudge the state of the in-coming tide, claim to have been warned against it by a sudden frantic shriek close at hand. This was attributed to the spirit of a wicked man, who drowned here while attempting to perform his very first good deed – summoning a priest to a dying woman's bedside. Thus his intended mission of mercy has been perpetuated, in warning others of the danger which claimed his own life.

Apart from the belief that the Gannel was haunted, local folk feared that a supernatural force might be unleashed if a certain field in the parish were to go under the plough. Centuries ago, it seems, carriers with pack mules converged on Bodmin offering for sale luxurious clothing at very low prices, before making a hurried departure. When the inhabitants suddenly sickened and died, word got around that the garments had been infected with the plague, and the victims' bodies were carted away and buried in a field at Crantock. This gruesome story gave rise to the fear that the angel of death would hover around if the hummocky land were ever to be disturbed.

Ecclesiastically, Crantock was a place of some importance from early times. A collegiate church was established on the site where St Carantocus had founded an oratory. The church perpetuates the theme of saints and sinners by depicting a saint standing in a niche, and a sinner sitting by the stocks. The latter was William Tinney, a smuggler's son who robbed a poor widow in 1817, and got his humiliating come uppance in this way.

The old manor house at Crantock is said to be haunted by a man of the cloth, one Dr Pusey. This learned theologian spent some time here and was wont to descend the steps to the shore and wander along the beach, deep in thought. When the manor was used as a guest house, some visitors were bemused by a shadowy figure seen pacing around at dusk, looking pre-occupied. One elderly lady who walked into the drawing room spoke to the rather strangely attired gentleman standing gazing out of the window and complained to the proprietor about the rudeness of her fellow guest in failing to reply. She was rather taken aback to be told that she was the only person staying there.

CUBERT

A profusion of small lanes converging on the pretty, windswept village of Cubert, to the north of Perranporth, gives an indication of its importance in earlier times, in an area much affected by the movement of sand. The nearby ancient oratory of St Piran became buried beneath the dunes of Penhale, in a wild and lonely environment haunted by seabirds and the spirits of those who lie buried in the sands.

Cubert's famous holy well in a cavern on the shore (where contraband goods were landed), was thought to have miraculous powers of healing. Annual fairs were held on Holywell beach on Holy Thursday, when the supernatural qualities of the water were at their most powerful. The celebrations included a ceremony which involved sliding sick children into the water through a cleft in the rocks.

The handsome spire on the tower of Cubert's church has served as a navigational aid to shipping for centuries. Smuggling was a thriving industry, indulged in by all layers of society. Indeed, it was placed on record that:

Cubert's vicar
Loves good liquor.

Contraband goods were concealed in various places, including the Smugglers Den Inn, where it is reported a customs officer was murdered after stumbling upon a consignment. Staff and customers have repeatedly experienced general feelings of being watched or followed, and unexplained voices have been heard after closing time. Perhaps it is the spectre of the murdered officer trying to catch out would-be smugglers.

There also seems to be a regular male ghost in the cellar area. A very cheeky one at

The Smugglers Den Inn, where the ghost of a boy cyclist, killed after colliding with the corner of the pub, has been seen.

that, as one member of staff even claimed that her bottom was pinched. Paranormal investigators claim it is the spirit of a lively fellow by the name of Alfred. They also picked up the spirit of a boy, which they linked to a bicycle accident about 60 years ago, when a rather backward child collided with the side of the building, with fatal consequences. An elderly female customer once asked the manager if the place was haunted because she could see an old lady with long grey hair and wearing a nightdress, sitting near the fireplace in a rocking chair.

Paul, the manager, remained somewhat sceptical about these supposed sightings until he experienced a strange encounter of his own: 'It was the end of a busy evening, I was here with a couple of members of staff and I was cashing up the till. The staff were sitting at the bar and I looked straight ahead of me into a dimly lit area of the dining room. I saw a lady sitting at table 18 and my first thought was that I had turned the lights out when a customer was clearly still sitting there. The lady was not a character from folklore, she wasn't faint or ghostly looking, she just sat at the table staring straight ahead. She appeared to be about 60 years old and wore a camel coloured coat with cream buttons. She had clearly had her hair done and was wearing make up. I looked away, convinced that my eyes were playing tricks and expected her to have vanished when I looked back, but she was still there. It was at this point that one of the girls sitting at the bar broke into my thoughts, concerned at the apparent lack of colour in my cheeks and drained expression. I looked at her and then back at the table but the lady was gone.'

LANHYDROCK

L anhydrock has a colourful history. It was originally owned by Bodmin Priory, but after the Dissolution of the Monasteries these lands were acquired by the neighbouring Glynn family. In 1620, the highly desirable estate was bought by Sir Richard Robartes.

The Roberts family of Truro, later Robartes, had risen to prominence in the 16th century after making their fortune as merchants and bankers, with interests in the tin trade. Sir Richard promptly set about building one of the most beautiful houses in Cornwall, a job completed by his son John after his father's death. John played a central role in the Civil War on behalf of the Parliamentarians and was later created Earl of Radnor. For a while the estate was in the hands of the Royalists. Although the king warned his troops to respect the properties of their enemies, one of his men was accused of looting at Lanhydrock and was hanged here. It is thought that the ghostly male figure often seen wafting around the vicinity of the gatehouse is the hapless thief.

John Robartes' second wife, Isabella, was considerably younger than her husband and bore him fourteen children. She was jealously guarded by her husband, and is thought to be the ghostly grey lady in full length dark apparel who roams the house. Some have seen her walking down the gallery or sitting in an armchair in the drawing room and have mistaken her for a real person until they watched her fade away.

Moving on to the next generation, the first Earl's eldest son Robert, Viscount Bodmin, became a Cornish MP, as did subsequent members of the family. Indeed his eldest son, Charles Bodville also became Lord Lieutenant. The house suffered a period of neglect in the 18th century but was revived after passing through the female line, when the U-shape of the building, which can still be seen today, was created.

Thomas James Agar-Robartes inherited the property from his mother in 1822. He was created Baron Robartes of Lanhydrock and Truro. The house was enlarged and outbuildings created, but fate dealt a terrible blow in April 1881 when fire gutted most of the house. The *West Briton* reported: '*As night came on, the scene was one of weird grandeur. Some of the timbers were still occasionally bursting into flame in the boisterous wind.*' Lady Robartes was rescued but died from the effects of the fire. Her husband was so overwhelmed by grief that he soon followed her to the grave. A strange and eerie female presence which has been felt rather than seen, has been linked to the tragic Lady Robartes.

Following the fire, the house was rebuilt, retaining some of its distinctive features, while incorporating the latest technology and fashions. In its heyday 25 staff were employed indoors and a further 70 around the Lanhydrock estate. But the First World War marked the end of the idyll when the eldest son was killed. It became a much quieter place and was inhabited by a surviving son and his two sisters. During the Second World War they took in evacuees and Lanhydrock once again echoed with the happy sounds of childhood. The house was given over to the National Trust in 1953.

Happier times at Lanhydrock are reflected in the sound of a little girl's laughter emanating from the Victorian nursery. There have also been reports of a phantom figure with a ruddy complexion in a fustian jacket and long waistcoat, hastily getting up from a crouching position in the billiards room, as if caught out doing something wrong. This area was formerly the brewhouse and it has been suggested that the guilty ghost may have been helping himself to a little tipple. The unexplained phenomena of whiffs of cigar smoke in the gentlemen's smoking room, when no one is around, also seems to be created by a spirit still hankering after earthly pleasures.

Paranormal investigators claim to have been in touch with several of the female servants, including one who fell down the stairs to her death, and another who hanged herself from a tree, having become pregnant whilst still single. Mediums who have visited have spoken of a male spirit who lived here in the mid-19th century, who met his death during a military campaign in India, and a contented one who died here at the age of 81, who still occupies a corner chair in the servants' quarters.

MORWENSTOW

From Padstow Point to Lundy Light,
Is a watery grave both day and night.
(Rev Robert Stephen Hawker)

The parish of Morwenstow lies in the far north of the county, in a sparsely populated area characterised by rolling farmland and small scattered settlements, with a high, dramatic coastline, notorious for its shipwrecks. The atmospheric churchtown, with its handsome former vicarage and

View of the treacherous shoreline from Hawker's Hut. (Eric Bird)

glebe farm, is strikingly situated above a long, wooded gorge in an environment dominated by towering cliffs. Its church is dedicated to St Morwenna who, according to legend, was one of 24 children belonging to King Broccan of Breconshire. It is said she used to pray that a church be established near 'yonder barbarous hill' otherwise known as the Henna Cliff. She was even thought to have helped in its construction, carrying a stone picked up from the shore on her head, for the font.

When the celebrated parson poet Robert Stephen Hawker arrived here in 1834, his flock consisted mainly of agricultural workers and 'a mixed multitude of smugglers, wreckers and dissenters of various hue'. This presented quite a challenge to this sensitive, idealistic man of the cloth, who could be a bit of a tearaway himself in some respects, with a penchant for outrageous practical jokes.

It had long been a tradition for folk in these isolated and impoverished coastal communities, where winter could be particularly harsh, to rush down to the shore when shipwrecks occurred, and help themselves to whatever they could. The shipwreck victims were unceremoniously cast into pits created just above the tide line and Parson Hawker was very concerned about the dignity of these hapless souls in death.

Hawker was theatrical in his preaching, wore exotic clothes, disliked taking the burial service, hated the colour black and was something of a mystic. He loved animals and believed they had souls. To him birds were ethereal creatures, cleaving the heavens and interacting with the angels. He thought that everyone had a guardian angel and attributed violent storms and other frightening happenings to the wrath of God. He scorned his parishioners' naïve beliefs in witchcraft and superstition, and their claims to have seen mermaids and pixies, which they took to be the souls of unbaptised children. But he believed in ghosts, and felt the area to be haunted by the unburied dead. He even claimed to have seen and spoken with St Morwenna on a number of occasions. 'I know Morwenna lies here,' he once confided. 'I have seen her, and she has told me as much; and at her feet ere long I hope to lay my old bones.' According to Hawker she had furnished him with texts for his sermons, which he often wrote in his cliff-top hideaway.

The conscientious parson's daily duties around the parish were very demanding, but it was the shipwrecks which caused him most anguish and distress. All too frequently the prevailing currents deposited the carnage on his coastal doorstep. He came to dread the sound of impending storms, fancying he could hear the anguished cries of dying seafarers in every gust of wind. When disaster struck, it fell to him and his parishioners to carry the mangled bodies up from the shore and await the coroner's authorisation for burial in the churchyard, where scores of them lie.

In his youth, Hawker had married a personable and cultured woman 21 years his senior. In his old age, he took a wife 40 years his junior. She bore him three daughters, the eldest of whom was christened Morwenna. His health began to deteriorate in the harsh winter of 1874 and he went to stay with his brother in Boscastle, hoping the change of air would do him good. He travelled on to Plymouth to seek further medical advice but unfortunately he died there and is buried in Plymouth cemetery. His tomb bears the enigmatic inscription taken from his works: 'I would not be forgotten in this land'.

Sadly, although he never achieved his wish to be buried in the churchyard at Morwenstow, some believe him to be there in spirit. His ghostly form has been seen standing at the head of the stone which covers his first wife's grave, gazing mournfully at the blank space beside her, where he hoped his name would be cut. His presence is also felt in the hut on the cliff-top, where in his lifetime he would sit gazing out to sea, seeking inspiration. It is said that his characteristic sighs and moans can still be heard above the sound of impending storms.

*   *   *

The picturesque and pleasing Bush Inn, constructed of stone and cob around a small courtyard and adjoining open common land, is deep-rooted in antiquity. It retains an engaging atmosphere of the past, with its low beams, open fireplaces, intimate nooks and crannies and interesting artefacts

The Bush Inn, Morwenstow.

on the walls. A Celtic cross set in the floor and a leper's squint are reminders of the days when the place served as a chapel, and afflicted outcasts could listen to services through the hole in the wall.

This unique establishment has borne witness to a very wide range of saintly and rumbustious human activity, and was once favoured by smugglers and wreckers. Some of the colourful goings on in days gone by are eerily re-echoed by the sound of ghostly footsteps, knocking noises on a door which no longer exists and fleeting sightings of shadowy figures. The inn is especially haunted by a weathered, salty character in old-fashioned attire, which retreats through the wall if challenged.

PADSTOW

The little town of Padstow is the focal point of an area rich in colourful folklore and legend, with a strong supernatural element. The landscape bears witness to human activity from early times, and the discovery of coins, ornaments and other artefacts over the centuries demonstrates trading links and the possibility of a Roman settlement here. The natural harbour was apparently able to accommodate large vessels until the build-up of sand known as the 'Doom Bar' blocked the entrance and collected a harrowing catalogue of shipwrecks. According to legend this capacious haven was formerly under the care of a mermaid (or merrymaid), who was mortally wounded by an arrow from the crossbow of a foolish fellow. Before disappearing into the murky waters she flung some sand into the air and uttered a curse that the port would henceforth be choked by these golden grains. It is said that the spirits of those who met their fate on the dreaded Doom Bar can be heard 'hailing their names'.

According to legend, the Doom Bar was created by a mermaid's curse.

The fisherfolk of old were very superstitious and lived in dread of hearing the 'calling of the dead'. During

Christmas 1848, when all the fishing boats except one were enjoying bountiful catches of herring, the fishing fraternity convinced the unlucky crew of this particular boat that their vessel was bewitched. This prompted them to nail a horseshoe to the keel, and the next night they too returned to port laden down with fish.

On another occasion, a cargo of pilchards brought ill-fortune to a farming family of Harlyn Bay, just west of Padstow. After Italian buyers had refused to pay the going price, the fish were dumped on one of the fields and the farmer refused to let the half-starved villagers help themselves. Subsequently, the local witch, Mother Ivey, put a curse on the field, whereby the eldest son of any family attempting to cultivate it would meet an untimely death. Soon afterwards the eldest son was thrown from his horse and died in the field, and the curse continued to reverberate down the years.

The London & South Western Railway finally arrived somewhat belatedly at Padstow in 1899 and was much used for the next 60 years. There was general dismay when a decision was made to close the line in 1966 and some people claim to have heard the sounds of a ghostly steam train rattling across the iron viaduct spanning Little Petherick Creek, on what has now become the Camel Trail. Generations of travellers approaching on the train which ran alongside the Camel estuary got their first cameo impression of Padstow nestling snugly by the water, backed by high ground, the plantation of Prideaux Place and the church tower rising in the centre.

*　　*　　*

The lands of Padstow once belonged to Bodmin Priory, and Prideaux Place occupies the site of a monastery destroyed by the warring Danes in AD 981. There have been reports of ghostly monks on the ancient route they once traversed between Padstow and Bodmin. At the time of Henry VIII, Nicholas Prideaux, aide to the dying Prior Vyvyan, ensured that the prior's successor would be William Munday, and was

Prideaux Place, considered to be one of Britain's most haunted houses.

The haunted staircase at Prideaux Place.

duly rewarded with the leases of tithes of four parishes, including Padstow. Realising that the wealthy priory was likely to have its lands seized by the king, he persuaded the prior to grant a long lease on the lands of Padstow to his niece. She then married his own nephew, and heir, thus securing the lands for the Prideaux family. The impressive castellated mansion constructed by Nicholas Prideaux's great nephew in 1592, was updated by Edmund Prideaux in the 18th century, who also landscaped the gardens.

Generations of the Prideaux family are recalled in the parish register, and ancestral portraits can be seen in the house today. The family had an upstanding reputation, with various members distinguishing themselves over the years as lawyers, MPs and in other worthy roles. One 16th-century Prideaux wife, however, is remembered for her bold and reckless behaviour. After the merchant ship *Mary Bonaventure* was seized by French pirates and then taken over by English privateers, the ship arrived in Padstow where part of the cargo was purchased by Richard Prideaux. They were illegal goods, however, and Richard was forced to flee from the authorities who eventually cornered him on board another vessel in Padstow harbour. Acting on impulse, his spirited wife leapt aboard flourishing a knife and promptly stabbed the senior commissioner. In the commotion that followed, a quick-witted local claimed that the authorities had murdered the poor lady and had them arrested. It was several days before it became clear that no such murder had been committed, by which time the cargo had vanished.

There have long been reports of apparitions at Prideaux Place, including at least one ghostly female. A few years ago an electrician was so scared by the sight of the phantom lady that he fled, and nothing would induce him to return to finish his task. Although legend associates this particular ghost with Honor Fortescue, who was said to have thrown herself over the balcony when her young husband died of smallpox, history tells rather a different story. In fact, there was no such balcony and she went on to remarry and have children, so who the phantom lady is remains a mystery.

Other supernatural happenings have occurred on the stairs and in various parts of the house over the years. In one particular bedroom, guests have been awoken by the barking or growling of an unseen dog, sometimes rather unnervingly from under the bed. Mediums on a recent television show considered Prideaux Place to be one of Britain's most haunted houses, and made particular mention of a Roman soldier, a monk and a highwayman, which would align with the history of the place.

Elizabeth Prideaux Brune has seen the figure of a boy walking across the stone-flagged scullery floor into the larder on several occasions. This is where my first attempt with divining rods came up with the letters FAUKL. I got a shock when I learnt that Fulke Prideaux Brune was the present owner's grandfather, and was shown his portrait in the hall.

*   *   *

Abbey House on North Quay, one of the oldest houses in Cornwall, was formerly in the possession of the Prideaux family. It is reputedly haunted by a lonely and forlorn woman of Elizabethan times, who comes up the staircase from the cellar then proceeds along a passage in the oldest part of the building.

*   *   *

Strange things also happened in the 16th-century former White Hart Inn, where mysterious footsteps passing at close quarters continued up the stairs and sounds resembling laboured breathing were heard. Milk bottles would rearrange themselves and a heavy oak door would burst open spontaneously and swing back and forth. Some men working there once saw two ghostly figures in an upstairs room when the place was unoccupied.

ST NEWLYN EAST

The delightful manor house of Trerice, romantically situated on the side of a luxuriant valley just north of St Newlyn East, exudes an engaging domestic atmosphere of the past, much to the delight of today's visitors. At the time of Domesday its name of Trevret signified a farm by a ford,

Trerice manor house.

and there have been a number of variations in the spelling since then. The little manor of Trerice had good arable and pastoral land, with the potential of promising mineral wealth lurking just beneath the surface. The story goes that John Coke, an artful Devon attorney-at-law, betrayed the trust of Sir Francis Godolphin, of nearby Helston, when managing his estates and mines, by stamping his own insignia on the mineral blocks instead of his employer's distinctive dolphins. He lined his own pockets to the extent that he was able to purchase Trerice and, to add insult to injury, married a Godolphin lady called Prudence, and had three sons. Although they did well, it was said that the sins of the grandfather were visited on his grandson Thomas, who slipped in a shallow pit and died whilst prospecting for tin. He was not the only person associated with Trerice whose fate was apparently predestined. Trerice came into the possession of the famous Arundel family in the 14th century when Ralph married Jane, the daughter and heiress of Michael Trerice. The manor house was constructed in the 1570s by Sir John Arundel, and the north wing was rebuilt in 1954, after having fallen into decay during the 19th century.

Having become heavily involved in politics and proved their worth on the battlefield, the Arundels acquired power and influence in Cornwall and much further afield. The Trerice branch of the family interacted with the rest of the gentry, made prudent marriages and increased their wealth. They had a penchant for naming their eldest sons John and, for over three centuries, the male heirs donned the demanding mantle created by their illustrious ancestors.

During the 15th century, Sir John Arundel had chosen to live on his pleasantly situated estate at Ebbford (Ebbing ford) near Stratton, where he had established a profitable salt water mill accessible over a causeway across the sands at low tide. But when a fortune-teller prophesied that he would meet his death on the sands, he hastily re-located to his inland property of Trerice, to avoid such a fate. When the news broke that St Michael's Mount was under siege by the Earl of Oxford, Edward IV proclaimed him a traitor and ordered Sir John, as Sheriff of Cornwall, to regain it. So he hastily raised an army and, on reaching the area, sent a trumpeter to the Earl summoning him to surrender the garrison to the king, hoping to avoid bloodshed. This was met with defiance, and in the course of the ensuing skirmish Sir John was slain on the sands at the foot of the Mount. He was buried in the chapel there. This uncanny sequence of events recalls the old proverb about fate foretold being likely to be fulfilled.

In 1664 the second son of Sir John Arundel was created Baron Arundel of Trerice. After the death of the 4th Lord Arundel in 1768, the estate passed to Sir Thomas Acland Dyke, a descendent of Margaret Arundel, whose monument and virtuous epitaph can be seen in St Newlyn East church.

There is a long-standing tradition that the ancient baronial mansion of Trerice is haunted by the spirit of a lecherous member of the Arundel clan, known locally as 'the Wicked Lord'. He is particularly associated with the rebuilt north wing. The ghostly grey lady, thought to be Margaret Arundel, is reported to walk there, as well as in the gallery and down the circular stone staircase. Various people have spoken of a shadowy figure with a flat-topped headdress wafting down the gallery, where one might fancy the personalities so powerfully portrayed in the paintings lining the walls may suddenly emerge from their frames, as in a scene from Gilbert & Sullivan's opera *Ruddigore*. A number of people have said that they felt uncomfortable in this area, and one female visitor who entered the gallery was unable to go any further. Some claim to have seen a phantom lady on the four-poster bed in the north chamber, while one of the guides refuses to go on duty in the court chamber, having experienced strong whiffs of a musky, lily-of-the-valley perfume, which fades away, giving her the sensation that some unseen person was walking past. This psychic fragrance has also been described by others as 'lilac like'. Spirits dislike being disturbed and, during the rebuilding of the north wing, some of the workmen became aware of an eerie swishing sound accompanied by a fragrance, giving the impression of a fine lady in crinoline skirts bustling past.

TINTAGEL

'The stranger, as he contemplates its mouldering, time-worn stones, will probably recall the romantic stories of King Arthur and his stalwart knights, and re-erect the castle 'in the air', gay with a pageant of ancient days, and echoing the wild music and clanking harness of warriors; for, in truth, the solitude and magnificence which now characterise the spot are well calculated to encourage a truant fancy.'
(*Handbook for Travellers in Devon & Cornwall*: 1865)

The romantic ruins of Tintagel Castle retain echoes of King Arthur. (Eric Bird)

Poets, dreamers and geologists have long been drawn to this spectacular section of coastline, where dark, high and mighty cliffs with topsy-turvy contortions are pounded by the relentless Atlantic rollers. It is a mystical, romantic environment steeped in folklore and legend.

Our forebears were wary of the fantastic array of fossils found in the rocks, and regarded ammonites as evil omens on account of their resemblance to coiled up serpents. They saw the butterfly-like fossils as symbols of eternal life. Some associated the dramatic rock formations and archaeological remains with giants, witches and wizards and whimsical goings on. Yet modern scientific theories on this hauntingly beautiful coastline could be regarded as equally magical. They tell us that those fossilised sea creatures once inhabited tropical seas and, furthermore, the movement of the earth's tectonic plates carried the equatorial land mass northwards to its present position on Cornwall's Atlantic coast, leaving imprints of primeval life, which existed long before mankind, suspended in the rocks.

These geological formations underwent a complete metamorphosis, having subsequently been covered by heavy layers of rock, and subjected to further earth movements, volcanic action and extremes of heat and cold, resulting in the twisting, folding, tilting and buckling of the land. Such a grandiose, elemental feat of Mother Nature would present quite a challenge to any giant, witch or wizard, in an environment where the physical and metaphysical seem to unite.

The grand and noble headland known as Tintagel Island was recognised as a natural fortress from earliest times, and successive generations incorporated the rock formations so cleverly that it is difficult to differentiate between art and nature amid the romantic ruins that we see today. It was a magnificent site fit for a king, in the days when warrior kings led their troops into battle.

A profusion of colourful myths and legends, with a strong supernatural element surround Tintagel Castle. Stories of Mark, his nephew Tristan and the beautiful Yseult were associated with this majestic site, but the most romantic and celebrated tales were woven around the noble and heroic King Arthur and his Knights of the Round Table, with their ideals of chivalry, gallantry and courtly love.

According to tradition, Uther Pendragon, King of Britain, invited the Cornish Duke Gorlois and his beautiful wife Igraine to a splendid feast at Winchester. When the Duke realised that the king was becoming infatuated with his fair lady's charms, he made a rapid return to Cornwall, and concealed her in a castle. The love-struck monarch pursued and slaughtered him, then with the assistance of the wizard Merlin disguised himself as the duke, and gained access to the marital bedchamber. The remarkable child born of this union was christened Arthur, instructed in worldly wisdom and groomed in knightly accomplishments throughout his formative years, to emerge as an idealistic, world famous hero.

Although it was stated in ancient times that 'the grave of Arthur no man knows', the Cornish would cite his burial ground at Slaughterbridge on the upper reaches of the River Camel, where he supposedly fought his last bloody battle. However, according to folklore, Arthur did not die; rather he was transformed into a Cornish chough (raven) by magical means, and was destined to return one day to reign again. He would recover his kingdom and sceptre and lead his people into a glorious age of peace and plenty. The red talons and beak of the chough, signifying blood, were thought to reflect his violent death. Local folk firmly believed that he haunted the battlements of his castle in the form of a bird and so refrained from killing any birds seen there.

There was also a long-held tradition that the castle walls were treated with magical paint, rendering it invisible one day a year, to briefly re-appear in all its ancient splendour. In more recent times some claimed to have glimpsed a ghostly Arthurian figure lurking amid the dark and crumbling ruins against an

The sound of ghostly subterranean bells recalls a vessel wrecked to the north of Tintagel, carrying the bells of Forrabury church.

atmospheric background of pounding waves, howling winds and plaintive cries of seagulls.

Many poets, writers and intellectuals have been drawn to this haunting environment, interpreting and embroidering the Arthurian legend in various ways. The influential occult philosopher Rudolph Steiner, founder of the Anthroposophy movement, who came here in 1924 and was struck by the spiritual and mystical significance of the legendary theme, saw it as the site of a Mystery School. He reckoned that the twelve main Arthurian characters reflected the zodiac, and served as channels for cosmic energy forces. Arthur, the central figure, represented the Sun, Guinevere the moon, while the rest were stellar knights. Their purpose was to influence the spiritual aspect of humanity.

The tower of the now isolated cliff-top church has served as an important landmark for seafarers for centuries along this stark and inhospitable coastline, and many victims of shipwreck were buried in its atmospheric churchyard. According to tradition the five bells which sang out so merrily from the distinctive square tower, were the envy of the folk of neighbouring Boscastle, who decided to have some fine bells made for the silent tower of their own church on the cliffs at Forrabury. The story goes that the vessel carrying the precious bells from London was wrecked on the rocks to the north of Tintagel, and that the sound of ghostly subterranean bells can be heard at the height of wild Atlantic storms. Some still claim to have heard the bells, and to have seen phantom boats rowed by phantom crews going to the aid of the ill-fated ship.

TRETHEVEY (ST NECTAN'S GLEN)

The impressive landscape around Trethevey (David's Place) to the north-east of Tintagel, seen to good effect from the commanding eminence of Condolen Barrow, harbours intriguing clues to former times, arousing our curiosity while leaving many questions unanswered. Tumuli, prehistoric tracks and mysterious maze carvings on a rock face in Rocky Valley, bearing a marked resemblance to the Galatian style of the Bronze Age, stimulate an awareness of the past.

The discovery of a granite milestone here in 1919, then serving as a gatepost but bearing an inscription to the Roman Emperors, Caesars and the lords Galius and Volusian, who reigned briefly between AD 251 and AD 253, implied a probable prestigious Roman connection with the renowned site of Tintagel Castle. There is a tradition that Trethevey had its own courthouse, and that a gallows or gibbet formerly stood by the highway, where a massive hedge dividing the parishes of Tintagel and Trevalga runs down the hillside to the coast. The tiny little church of St Piran, with its fascinating frescoes and

Many weird and wonderful stories have surrounded St Nectan's Glen – and continue to do so. (Truro Museum)

holy well, and the possible site of a former hermitage above St Nectan's Kieve, provide a long-established religious perspective on what many people regard as a deeply spiritual environment.

Our early forebears and missionary saints established settlements in places favoured with a good water supply. Water had a profound sacred and symbolic significance and here they were blessed with a profusion of springs contributing to the busy little river which tumbles through the Trevillett valley before veering northwards to meet the sea. The upper part of the valley is well wooded, with a narrow chasm, in which a waterfall cascades through a cleft in the high vertical rock face into a naturally occurring basin known as St Nectan's Kieve.

The haunting beauty of St Nectan's Glen, with its focal point the dramatic waterfall and kieve, gave rise to a profusion of wonderful myths and legends about King Arthur and his knights, druids, monks, nuns, mysterious maidens, mariners and their ghosts and priceless treasures. This remarkable place captured the imagination of a number of 19th-century writers and artists, including Wilkie Collins, Dickens, Thackeray and the Rev Stephen Hawker. The artist Daniel Maclise felt moved to produce a painting of the semi-divine maiden he fancied he saw in the shimmering spray of the waterfall, which was exhibited at the Royal Academy in 1843.

The Glen, which has been designated a Site of Special Scientific Interest, is regarded as one of Cornwall's most sacred shrines, with the remarkable font-like formation of the kieve being of particular significance. According to tradition this was where King Arthur and his knights met, and where they were baptised before setting out on their quest to discover the Holy Grail. People continue to be drawn here in search of spiritual revitalisation and fulfilment.

Ruins of the building found further up the fern-covered banks of the waterfall were taken to be those of the dwelling of a pious hermit called St Nectan, after whom the place is named. It is said that those wending their way up to the hermitage and waterfall today are following the path used by generations of pilgrims who came to worship at his shrine. He prayed for the welfare of seafarers, and was wont to ring a silver bell in a nearby tall tower to warn them of impending danger. This devout man of simple faith fell out with passing strangers over religious matters, and shortly before his death he decided to dispose of the priceless bell in the deep recesses of the waterfall, so that non-believers would never be able to get their hands on it. He requested that he be laid to rest along with sacramental vessels and other treasures in an oaken chest, within splashing range of his beloved waterfall. Several centuries later some foolish miners made attempts to recover this valuable hoard but took to their heels and fled when an eerie voice warned them, 'The child is not born who shall recover this treasure!' Furthermore, bad luck would befall anyone hearing the ghostly ringing of the silver bell.

Stories about St Nectan and his followers were linked with that of two enigmatic, elderly sisters with an air of faded gentility, who suddenly appeared on the scene and dwelt here as recluses. Some have associated the sisters with the ghostly grey ladies of Genver Lane. Reports of ghostly goings on in this magical place, where a sense of other worldliness is heightened by the heady, hypnotic sound of running water have proliferated since Victorian times, when it was thought to be haunted by monks. In more recent times local people and walkers claim to have heard the sound of chanting monks, and seen them moving along singly or in small groups. They were generally thought to be kindly disposed, rather than inspiring fear and some walkers say they have been accompanied by ghostly monks on their way through the glen. The overall sensation is that of not being alone.

Apart from the traditional monks, nuns, bards, druids and mariners who may have met their doom on this rocky shoreline after the demise of the watchful saint, there were reported sightings of piskies, believed to encompass the spirits of stillborn children. A ghostly dog is thought to patrol the path through the woods, while various canines and cats have been known to start behaving strangely, as if responding to some unseen threat. Other weird experiences attributed to the supernatural include fragments of music reminiscent of a chapel organ issuing from a deserted building, eerie whispering, heartfelt sobbing erupting into chilling, cynical laughter, and the sound of following footsteps when no one is there.

•West Cornwall•

CAMBORNE

The historic Cornish Choughs at Treswithian.

The once thriving town of Camborne seems to have been the focus of some unusual and very disconcerting supernatural manifestations. A well known 19th-century mine captain told of his encounter with three female spirits in Truthall Lane one dark evening. In response to his polite greeting, they kept chanting in doom-laden tones: 'The living have naught to do with the dead ...' Whereupon he took to his heels, and made sure he never passed that way after nightfall again.

The nearby hamlet of Crane was also haunted by spirits, who were much feared by the older folk after dark. The trouble centred around the ghost of an old mine captain, who had been a great trader in shares. After his death he continued to sit in the doorway of his office, doing business with ghostly customers. The local folk were relieved when Parson Richards came on the scene, with his ghost-laying skills.

On one occasion when the curate of Camborne was carrying out a midnight ritual in the south porch of the church, with a prayer book in one hand, a candle in the other and a horsewhip hanging over his shoulder, he was disturbed by two miners from Treswithian returning home via the churchyard footpath. As they pressed forward to speak to him he swung round in fury, exclaiming, 'Why did 'ee 'ave to go an' break the spell like that? Two minutes more an' I should've 'ad 'un fast in hell! Who knows when I shall catch 'un again?' And in his frustration he grabbed his horsewhip and chased them all the way home.

An inn or hostelry, variously known as the Cornish Daws, Cornish Choughs, Three Cornish Choughs or the Choughs has stood at the crossroads of Treswithian (known locally as Jethan) for centuries. Treswithian, documented as Trevaswethan in 1292, was a small manor within the larger manor of Tehidy, owned by the Basset family who made their fortune out of mining. Ken Bowden, who took over the pub in 1981, reckoned that it was 406 years old at that time, although little of the original fabric remains. He explained that it was on the route of the old copper-carrying mule trains plying between Redruth and the port of Hayle, with the advantage of having a reliable well. There must have been some lively goings-on at this convenient overnight stop for these rough and ready characters and their beasts of burden. This route attracted more travellers when it was incorporated in the busy highway which later became the A30, with a variety of horse-drawn and motor vehicles calling here. The place was run by the Rowe family, assisted by two servants and an ostler from the mid 19th century until 1909, and it was run by the Manhires, Pascoes, Kanes and Bowdens after that.

The Kanes, who ran the pub from 1968 until 1981, became aware of strange happenings after making alterations to the downstairs bars and an upstairs bedroom in order to create an additional staircase. One night after closing time when Jean Kane was alone in the pub, her eye fell on an old rail with square pegs, and she experienced an awareness of the days when coaches and horses arrived here, and hardy drivers would come stomping in out of the cold throwing their coats up on those time-worn wooden pegs. Then she experienced a really weird feeling, like an icy arm going round her back. The temperature suddenly dropped and it felt incredibly cold. She remained rooted to the spot and, when her husband returned from walking the dog, she told him that she thought they had 'company', and explained what had happened. At various times after that the dog would react to a seemingly unseen presence coming through that large door. His fur would stand on end, and he would leap and snatch at something.

An abiding feature associated with strange happenings at the Choughs, and which had also been there for centuries, was the old fire grate with a connecting spit revolved by an elaborate clockwork device. On one occasion several people were surprised to see a white mouse running along the cord of the clockwork mechanism. It disappeared, never to be seen again, and there were wisecracks about phantom mice and Dickory Dock. They came to regard this fire grate, originally situated in the kitchen, as being haunted by a spirit who was a bit of a teaser. The fire would die right down in the evening with every appearance of being burnt out, then blaze away hours later when there was nothing combustible in the grate. Objects would suddenly burst out from the fire. On one famous occasion, which happened to be on 31st October, a circular wooden section of an old bar stool placed in the fire and held down by a square poker shot out of the fire and remained poised on the top of the old round brass fender.

Such indefinable spookiness gave way to visual manifestations when the Kanes' daughter Bridget started to see a ghostly figure in her bedroom, sitting in the sunken section of an old-fashioned chest of drawers as if it were an armchair. The extraordinary thing was that this stockily-built apparition with a fresh complexion and receding hairline bore an uncanny resemblance to Dick Eddy, one of the regulars from the farm opposite. After Bridget got married and left, the ghostly old man continued to sit at the foot of the bed all night long, which was somewhat alarming for the various lodgers and bed and breakfast guests who occupied the room over the years. The son of the Bowdens, who took over from the Kanes, had a similar sighting, and shortly afterwards one of two small boys sleeping in another bedroom insisted that there was an old man sitting at the foot of his bed. These overnight visitors from up-country could have had no prior knowledge of the phantom guest.

The aforementioned Dick Eddy was himself philosophical about the supernatural happenings in the hostelry. He often recounted his experience of seeing the circular section of wood flying out of the fire and balancing on the fender. He got another shock when a customer making his way to the toilet spoke to a figure in the closed lounge bar, sitting by the empty grate. Much to his amazement the customer saw Eddy on his return and expressed his astonishment at seeing him sitting there when 'I have just been talking to you in the other bar!' Having a ghostly manifestation of yourself haunting a favourite place before you die really does show commitment!

CHYSAUSTER

The Romano-Cornish village of Chysauster, on the flank of a hill beneath the Iron Age fort of Castle-an-Dinas, is the best known of a host of prehistoric settlements in the granite landscape near Land's End. The houses are cleverly designed to provide maximum protection from wind and weather, while commanding extensive views of Mount's Bay and the surrounding countryside.

Trees which once covered these hillsides were cleared away by early settlers, who constructed shelters, grew crops and relied on wild and domestic animals. The first occupation of this site could have been connected with the fogou, a mysterious underground chamber which could have been used for storage, or possibly as a place of refuge from warring tribes. The present walled ruins are thought to date from the 2nd or 3rd centuries AD, when the Romans were in occupation. At one time the settlement was quite extensive.

The Cornish had long enjoyed trading links with the Mediterranean countries, whose vessels called at ports including St Michael's Mount, in quest of tin. They were used to interacting with foreign seafarers, and were regarded as civilised. The Romans, who pressed westwards into Cornwall, apparently co-existed with the Cornish tribes, who absorbed some of their culture and ideas. The influence of Roman forms can be seen in the distinctive pottery found here, described as 'Romano-British' ware. One Italian visitor declared that this courtyard village bore a marked resemblance to one she knew in Tuscany. The particular style is confined to this area and the Isles of Scilly, incorporating carefully planned drainage systems.

The oval rooms of the houses, constructed around an inner courtyard, had turfed or thatched roofs supported by central poles with corbelled stone roofs covering smaller areas. There were individual garden plots and long terraced fields along the hillside. The inhabitants may have carried out some tin streaming in the valley to the west, but this was

The Romano-Cornish village at Chysauster, where some have experienced echoes of the past.

primarily a farming community. They would have kept cattle, sheep, goats and pigs, growing cereals and other crops.

In prehistoric times the place would have been a hive of industry, with people grinding corn, weaving cloth and fashioning pots. Reports of small ghostly figures seen running around the ruined houses have been associated with those early inhabitants. There have also been sightings of a ghostly watcher on the hill, maintaining vigilance across the centuries and keeping an eye on our comings and goings. One psychic said he was aware of being alongside the watcher, who was with a woman with a broken arm and a child. One of the custodian's dogs is in the habit of focusing on this high point and barking when there is no one about. This dog also reacts to Hut 6, where there has been a claimed sighting of a warlike figure. Paranormal experts have had positive responses in some of the other huts, and mention has been made of a cat and a cow. Most agree that there is considerable activity associated with this site, which has a peaceful and benign aura.

LAND'S END

The appearance of a white hare is to fishermen a foreboding of storms, and they dread to walk at night near those parts of the shore where wrecks have occurred, as the souls of drowned sailors appear to haunt the scene, and the voices of the dead can be heard at times mingling with the noise of the waves. Should a cloud of misty vapour assume a peculiar form, the fishermen say it is a spirit sent to warn them against venturing to sea, by the kindly interposition of some ministering angel. In the parish of St Levan, it is believed there can be seen at times a spectre ship, which appears to be sailing over the land; this is considered a sign of bad luck to the beholder.
(Mrs Henry Pennell, *Bygone Days in Devonshire and Cornwall*, 1874)

The coastal waters around the exposed promontory of Land's End, which takes the full force of wind and waves and variable weather, have been notorious among mariners the world over for centuries; for this was awesome shipwreck territory, where countless seafarers have met their doom. The unyielding coastline continues to collect casualties, even in this sophisticated hi-tech age.

Henri Alphonse Esquiros, a French professor who had a great empathy with Cornwall and its people, wrote in 1865: 'Shipwrecks in these seas, bristling with

Looking out across the Lost Land of Lyonesse.

reefs, were not only very numerous some years ago, but they had a particularly grave character. A ship was crushed by dashing against rocks or precipices. What was this ship? Ask this of the winds, the sea, the few insignificant fragments tossing on the immensity of the waves. To die unknown is dying twice over. Such was the lot of many ships, and no one ever knew their name, their country or the number of passengers on board.'

It is hardly surprising that folk in this harsh and isolated environment should adhere to the age-old belief that souls in anguish could be heard 'hailing their names' above the sound of raging storms and it was customary to throw fish into the sea as offerings to the Bucca Dhu and Bucca Gwidden (black and white spirits).

According to local tradition, Porthcurno, formerly known as Port Curnoe (Cove of Horns or Corners), was the principal port of Cornwall until the navigable channel extending to the head of the creek became choked with sand. In this area of violent storms and sudden descent of sea mist, it was claimed that a ghostly black square rigger came in from the sea and proceeded across the sands and up the valley.

Although fleets of spectre ships were thought to have manifested themselves during the port's heyday, to warn of impending enemy attack and reflect the strength of their force, appearances of a lone square rigger came to be associated with the family who dwelt at Chegwidden, a mile or so up the valley. The story goes that the drunken behaviour of Old Martin and the cruelty his second wife inflicted on his children caused his eldest son, who was named after him, to run away to sea. As the years rolled by it was assumed that Young Martin had been the victim of a shipwreck.

At harvest time some years later, workers in the fields noticed a large vessel approaching, which hove to while two men came ashore in a small boat laden with chests and other goods. There was great excitement when it became known that the wanderer had returned, albeit with a mysterious dark and swarthy companion called Jose, who spoke in a foreign tongue.

Martin soon discovered that the happy companions of his childhood had changed after coming under the influence of a strict religious sect. For their part local folk disapproved of his worldly ways, and were suspicious about Jose and how they had acquired so much wealth. However, the two men found a loyal ally in Martin's distant cousin, Eleanor. After having made unexplained overnight expeditions in their small boat, and acquired an impressive sailing vessel in which they disappeared to sea for months on end, it was rumoured that they were pirates, and some believed that they were in league with the devil.

Martin eventually fell ill, and as death approached he persuaded Jose to take him off to sea, hoping no doubt to make it to Fiddler's Green, the Sailors' Heaven. He cursed anyone who defied his wish not to be buried alongside his family in the churchyard at St Levan. Although local folk attended a burial service there, it was rumoured that the coffin was filled with earth, and that Jose had placed Martin's remains in a chest, along with all his worldly goods, before setting sail with Eleanor and Martin's favourite dog.

They were scarcely a league out to sea when a great tempest arose, which continued for a week. This is supposedly when Porthcurno's navigable creek was overcome by sand, and no vessel, apart from a phantom ship, ever entered the port again. She first appeared shrouded with mist soon after the storm subsided, when folk fancied they saw the shadowy figure of two men, a woman and a dog on the deck. This ship of the dead with its ghostly crew hovered over the sands, then drifted eerily inland towards Chegwidden before evaporating by a rock, where a hoard of coins was said to have been discovered many years ago. Although people may have been eager to catch a glimpse of the phantom ship, it is said to bring misfortune to the beholder.

The flat-topped altar tomb in St Levan churchyard of Captain Richard Wetherall, who lost his life when his brig *Aurora* was wrecked off the

Runnelstone in 1811, reputedly exudes the eerie sound of a tolling ship's bell from time to time. The story goes that the captain struck the bell eight times as the ship went down, hence the tradition was born that seafaring men would hear the muffled sound of eight bells just before their life's 'watch' ended.

Ghostly maritime bells from the land are complemented by the sound of phantom church bells under the sea, emanating from the legendary Lost Land of Lyonesse, between Land's End and the Isles of Scilly. Folk have long described hearing the sound of the splendid city's numerous church bells pealing in conditions of exceptional calm. Indeed, fishermen of old claimed to have seen submerged rooftops, and some of today's visitors are adamant that they have experienced mirages of the land that used to be.

At Sennen Cove, on the northern side of the Land's End peninsula, a rock called the Irish Lady marks the site of a shipwreck, from which she was the sole survivor. It is said that she returns to the rock in advance of storms, holding a rose between her teeth as a warning to mariners. The apparition of a lady carrying a lantern, supposedly searching for her child who was drowned, while she was saved, also foretells disaster at sea.

*   *   *

A succession of landlords of the First and Last Inn up at Sennen Churchtown, where smuggling activity proliferated, have reported various ghostly happenings in the hostelry. Most of these seem to be associated with the notorious Anne George, who once ran the inn with her husband Joseph, and had betrayed members of the Moonlight Brigade on several occasions. The couple acted as agents for their landlord Dionysius Williams, and blackmailed him by refusing to pay their rent. But when he evicted them, Anne George turned King's Evidence, and Williams was sentenced to a long term of imprisonment.

She paid a high price for violating the free trading fraternity's loyal code of conduct, for her former associates captured her, tied her to a stake at Sennen

The First and Last Inn at Sennen.

Cove and left her to her fate on the incoming tide. Her body was carted back to the inn and laid out in an upstairs bedroom before being interred in an unmarked grave in the adjacent churchyard.

New tenants Neil and Lynne Forster had a spectral welcome when they took over the inn in the autumn of 2004. Neil was keen to make use of the biggest of the four bedrooms, although his wife had an uneasy feeling about it. On the first evening the bedroom door inexplicably slammed shut behind her, and she suddenly felt very cold. When she mentioned this at the bar, a customer remarked that it was probably Anne George, her early 19th-century predecessor, but she dismissed the notion.

That night Lynne suddenly awoke, unable to move, while Neil was having a nightmare about being trapped in a net, and was thrashing about and screaming. Then she became aware of a ghostly black figure, which could have been male or female, standing at the bedside. On the second night she felt 'strange and cold'. On the third night she saw the ghost of Anne quite clearly as she entered the bedroom. She was standing in a corner in long dark apparel, and had a rather time-worn face. On the fourth night Lynne awoke feeling stifled, and was unable to move her arms. She experienced the sensation of water pouring across her face, and had an impression of a shoreline in the distance. The Forsters turned on the lights and everything returned to normal; although the next morning they were perplexed to discover one of their cats in a closed drawer, and another in a closed wardrobe.

They changed bedrooms after that and their nights have become less dramatic. Although Neil has never seen the phantom himself, he is aware of inexplicable happenings, while Lynne continues to have regular sightings of the notorious lady who paid the price for her betrayal.

MULLION

Mullion, on the western side of the Lizard, lies in an area steeped in antiquity and associated with fishing, smuggling, wrecking, saving lives, wartime airfields and an eccentric 17th-century ghost-laying parson. This stunningly beautiful coastline was the scene of many a cruel shipwreck in the days of sail, when vessels were driven on shore in the maritime trap of Mount's Bay. Many of the victims lie buried in the churchyard.

At a time when it was believed that spirits freely roamed the countryside, the Rev Thomas Flavel became incumbent here. This staunch Royalist, who had allowed his beard to continue growing until the return of the king to the throne in 1660, had a knack of communicating with the 'other side', and seemed to be on intimate terms with unseen powers. Whilst preaching in the church one day, he received word that something was amiss at the vicarage. He halted the service, dismissed the congregation and rushed home. When he got there he found that a prying servant girl, who had been foolish enough to open up one of his necromantic books, was being pinched and punched by a host of spirits which had suddenly encompassed her. He soon had the situation under control, however, and grasping the offending book, he read out backwards the magical words which had released them and swung his stick around. It did the trick and the spirits promptly vanished.

The parson's reputation as an exorcist spread like wildfire throughout the neighbourhood, where ghosts, pixies, witches and the devil himself sought mischief. On one occasion, when he demanded the extortionate fee of £5 for laying a ghost in a neighbouring churchyard, two curious petitioners thought they would get their money's worth and hid behind a gravestone at the appointed hour. They got more than they bargained for when they heard him crack his whip, and saw an eerie form peering at them from behind the opposite tombstone, before quitting its earthly prison.

There were those who believed that Thomas Flavel himself re-appeared here 150 years after his death, and that the parson of the time, who was also an exorcist, was obliged to lay his spirit to rest.

A profusion of tumuli in this area, where urns and human remains were discovered in the 19th century, probably contributed to the belief that some tracts of land were cursed. A field at Predannack known as Vaunder has never been ploughed or disturbed, for fear of bringing death or some other dire misfortune to the person responsible.

There is a tradition that three lepers escaping from a shipwreck found their way to Predannack Manor, where there was an ancient chapel, and that two of them were interred in the burial plot known as Jarine. It was generally thought that if ever this ground were to be disturbed, one of the occupants of the estate would die before the year was out. Indeed, when a Mullion man was murdered on his way home from Helston in 1820 it was attributed to the fact that the plot had recently been disturbed.

A prolonged, particularly bizarre supernatural manifestation occurred in a field between Mullion Air Station (at Bonython) and the village during the First World War. On 15th October 1917, when off-duty, Sub Lieutenant Jelf was on his way to visit friends in Mullion, he paused to look over a farm gate. There in the field he was appalled to witness a duel taking place, with the combatants flourishing rapiers and wearing what appeared to be Stuart costume. He was even more horrified when one of the contestants was run through, and the second brought up a coffin. The serviceman passed out when the victor suddenly pointed his sword at him. When he regained consciousness, he was lying on the ground by the gate and the field was empty.

Although friends attributed this to an hallucination brought on by pressure of work, Jelf remained adamant that this had been a supernatural occurrence and placed it on record in the library of the Royal Institution of Cornwall in Truro. Some years later a local vicar witnessed the chilling, ghostly sequence of events at the exact same spot. But nobody knows the origin of the phantom duellists.

PENZANCE

The sweeping northern shoreline of Mount's Bay, dominated by the romantic eminence of St Michael's Mount and protected by a hinterland rich in archaeological remains, is steeped in colourful history and folklore. It had always been vulnerable to attack by sea, and pirates sometimes came ashore to seize victims to be sold into slavery.

Penzance, which originated as a tiny fishing settlement clustered around an ancient chapel, developed into a busy port and market centre for the west of

Penzance harbour, 1860, where the appearance of a phantom dog foretold of disaster at sea.

Cornwall. Although traditionally frequented by rollicking seafaring characters, it became a cultural centre at the time of Sir Humphry Davy, attracting leading scientific figures of the day and fashionable folk in the late 18th and early 19th centuries.

The Dolphin Inn in Dock Street, well known to generations of seafarers, remains the scene of unexplained phenomena. The place is traditionally associated with Sir John Hawkins, who reputedly used it as his headquarters while rallying men to crew the ships at the time of the Spanish Armada, and the notorious Judge Jeffries, who used the building as a courthouse in the 17th century and confined prisoners in the cellars. The place was strongly involved with smuggling activities, and when repairs were being carried out some years ago, a smugglers' hideaway was discovered, along with two casks in a good state of preservation. On a subsequent occasion, when a bedroom was being redecorated after a fire, a concealed door was found to lead to a secret room in the roof.

Over the years, members of staff have been aware of ghostly goings on, the sounds of eerie whispering and mysterious footsteps, and of being touched on the shoulder by an invisible hand. Heavy dragging noises as if furniture were being hauled across a wooden floor, evoke images of consignments of bulky contraband goods known to have been handled here. Could the smugglers of yore, who may have developed a taste for finery, have anything to do with the perplexing situation in bedrooms 4 and 5, where human imprints have been left on chairs, beds and pillows when the rooms are empty and locked? On one occasion a ghostly fair-haired young man was said to have been seen in one of the bedrooms. In recent times a ghostly woman in a dun coloured dress was seen to waft across the pool room.

The forbidding atmosphere of the cellar, with its shadowy forms, makes the staff very uneasy and some are reluctant to go down there at all. It is made all the harder by the knowledge that in 1873 an unfortunate young men fell to his death in that very spot. A number of people claim to have heard the sound of heavy footsteps moving from the front to the rear of an upstairs room, sometimes continuing down the stairs. This spook with a manly tread may be the one which occasionally manifests itself in the form of a bewhiskered ancient mariner, decked out in a tricorn hat, smart frilly shirt and tailored coat with brass buttons. This popular ghostly character is known to one and all as 'the Cap'n'. It is presumed that he met his death within these walls in dubious circumstances.

Those who spent their lives at sea were well aware of the daily hazards, and the sighting of a phantom black dog on the South Pier of the harbour was an ill omen. The shoreline could be quite an eerie environment at night. To the east, at Marazion Green, travellers on foot feared the ghostly white lady who would suddenly appear and glide along beside them for some distance, before slowly fading away. She was also said to leap onto the backs of horses being ridden across Marazion Marsh.

Rough and ready characters in 18th-century attire, allegedly seen humping crates up the slipway adjoining the Dry Dock in the direction of Chapel Street, evaporate if challenged. Nearly all the buildings in this fascinating street, where a number of houses occupy the sites of earlier structures, have laid claim to being haunted at one time or another. Chapel Street was where professional people lived, and where high-class craftsmen and traders plied their trade in the late 18th and 19th centuries. This was a compact, vibrant community, with a church, chapel, theatre and assembly rooms. The prestigious street was also a busy thoroughfare with daily mule trains, consisting of 70 or 80 pack animals carrying heavy loads of copper, causing quite a commotion as they made their way down to the quay for smelting.

Chapel Street in Penzance is reputed to be the most haunted street in the country.

There were regular funeral processions to St Mary's church, which replaced the earlier Chapel of St Mary in 1832, and it was customary for the town crier to perambulate the streets on Sundays, summoning worshippers by ringing his bell. The street also saw miscreants who had been confined in the stocks in the old chapel yard heading homewards, draped in white sheets and carrying lighted candles.

Legends about a phantom coach drawn by headless horses rumbling through the streets, and ghostly funeral processions wending their way to the church seem to re-echo past scenes in this historic place. Local folk stopped taking short cuts through the churchyard after reports of a ghostly figure flitting amongst the tombstones, and doleful noises issuing forth. A visiting seafarer who was confronted by the apparition let fly with his fists, and the figure left struggling on the ground turned out to be a Captain Carthew, a colourful character with a taste for jolly japes, not an apparition at all.

The wealthy Baines family occupied a substantial brick-built residence with a fine orchard in the early 19th century. After her husband died, Mrs Baines became increasingly troubled by local lads scrumping her apples. So, to combat this problem, she and her manservant Jan took it in turns to keep watch in the orchard overnight. Suspecting that he was not as vigilant as he might be, she crept downstairs in her nightgown to make sure he was being an effective guardian of her orchard. But as there was no sign of him, she shook the apples from her favourite apple tree, with the intention of accusing the poor fellow of allowing folk to make off with her finest produce. Hearing the noise, Jan, who had been taking a nap under the hedge, leapt to his feet and blasted a shot with his blunderbuss. The old lady was mortally wounded, and after her death a ghostly figure in a lace bonnet, full-length gown and silken mantle, effectively deterred any future would-be scrumpers.

The house remained empty for many years, after successive tenants were troubled by fleeting shadows flitting from room to room, and manifestations of the old lady working away at her spinning wheel. Some believed that she was condemned to spin black wool into white for eternity.

Although it was said that the restless spirit of Mrs Baines had been exorcised by the parson, it seems she continued to haunt her former home. She is also said to haunt the Turk's Head Inn where a number of unexplained things have happened over the years. Several restaurants and commercial premises have attributed supernatural goings on to a ghostly old lady, and cited her. There have also been sightings of a grey-haired old lady in a rocking chair at the old vicarage, and more recently in the window of an antiques shop. Wherever she is spotted, she manages to vanish in a trice.

An effigy of a smuggler on the rooftop of the Admiral Benbow, phantom forms in dark recesses, sounds of heavy footsteps and other eerie noises recall the boisterous days of old, but the pub's most enduring ghost is the gentle Annabelle, who died of a broken heart when her true love was lost at sea. Her sad figure can occasionally be seen at an upper window, as if waiting for the sailor who would never return. Staff say they have felt her presence down in the cellars, and barmen have felt her reassuring touch on their shoulder when things are quiet.

PERRANZABULOE PARISH
(ZELAH, VENTONGIMPS, MITHIAN)

The landscape around Mithian and Zelah was the scene of great prehistoric activity, with a profusion of earthworks and tumuli, while Lambourne Castle and the twin forts of Caer Dane and Caer Kief above the stream which reaches the sea at Perranporth are an indication of tribal strife in pursuit of power and territory. These lands were to see great mining activity in the 19th century, and glimpses of fleeting forms might be attributed to warriors slaughtered in battle or victims of mining accidents. At Ventongimps there are tales of a phantom horse which gallops across the terrain in endless pursuit of its rider killed in combat. There is a long-held tradition that a miner, who met his death in the famous West Chyverton lead and silver mine, haunts the dark and forbidding area of Chyverton Woods near Cotton Springs.

According to folklore, an old woman who came upon a set of teeth protruding from the soil in Perranzabuloe churchyard took them home and put them in her bedroom, thinking that they might come in useful. That night she heard a ghostly voice pleading 'Give me back my teeth! Give me back my

What caused the mark on this picture of Chyverton Woods?
Was it a faulty camera or a supernatural presence?

teeth!' from just below the window. Without daring to look outside, the terrified woman flung them out, whereupon the crying ceased, and she heard the sound of footsteps retreating in the direction of the churchyard. She got up early next morning to carry out a search, but found no sign of teeth, nor any trace of footprints.

The famous Miners' Arms at Mithian, where there have been some recent spooky goings-on, is steeped in history and harbours a few strange secrets. This building was originally part of Mithian Manor, first documented in 1201 and occupied by a French nobleman at one time. According to a decorative plaster ceiling, the Miners' Arms, which in the 19th century was listed as a public house, dates from 1577. The discovery of a secret tunnel which linked it with Mithian Manor, now a complex of houses, has led to the suggestion that it might have been a hiding place or escape route for persecuted priests or monks after the Reformation in the mid 16th century. It is said that the bones of a monk and fragments of his apparel have been discovered in the mysterious tunnel, which may have been connected with an earlier building on the site. Mithian Manor had once been in the possession of the Catholic Winslade family, who took part in the Prayer Book Rebellion of 1549.

This complex of buildings has been put to various uses in its long history and has witnessed some less than saintly happenings, particularly in the late 19th century, when it was closed down as a house of ill repute. At that time the buildings incorporated a couple of shops. There was a fairly rapid turnover of landlords until 1919, some of whom were in trouble for drunkenness themselves or for allowing drunkenness on the premises.

The Miners' Arms became the pub with no beer during the Second World War, when the demand from the RAF personnel billeted around the area exceeded supply. Part of the building became officers' quarters. Somewhat illogically, the landlady of the time disapproved of young servicewomen drinking at the bar.

When workmen carried out renovations to the pub in the late 1940s, they realised that the stone breastwork of the bar's open fireplace was too extensive to be solid. Further investigation revealed a secret room. There was another fireplace back to back with the one in the bar, and some stone steps leading down to a collapsed tunnel. The locals showed them the blocked-up entrance to a tunnel in the roadside embankment below the pub, which aligned with it, and one of them mentioned a former squire who had been executed for sheltering priests. Perhaps the most intriguing thing was the discovery of a lady's dainty leather shoe, with a heel and lace holes up the front. When one of the workmen returned 40 years later he was disappointed to find no trace of the concealed chamber, which seemed to have been swallowed up during extensive renovations, causing him to wonder whether subsequent disturbances might be associated with a secret Cinderella.

Although there had been a number of unexplained occurrences over the years, these seem to have intensified after the renovations of the 1960s. Several people were aware of an uneasy presence in one of the bedrooms, which one former landlady felt unable to enter. One guest said he had received a blow on his back as he walked downstairs, and the young children living there talked about a ghostly figure. Glasses would fall from the shelf for no apparent reason and remain unbroken on the hard floor. Sachets of sauce which had been neatly arranged the night before, would be unaccountably strewn across the floor the next morning.

Things got a bit hectic after a new landlady took over early in 2005. One of the regulars said he had seen chairs being thrown across the room when no one was there, and another said he was showing a couple of friends round the pub when a knife suddenly shot out of a drawer and struck one of them on the leg. The landlady's daughter was struck by a candlestick holder. The landlady, decided to seek the help of the church in putting to rest the troublesome spirit, which was frightening people. But a couple of days later the pub was struck by a fire, apparently caused by a spark in a dried out chimney. Two regulars ran in to tell them the roof was on fire, and the customers fled, leaving their drinks behind them.

Shortly afterwards the pub was visited by the Bishop of Truro's licensed Adviser of the Ministry of Deliverance, who quietens spirits and tries to remove difficulties that may be causing trouble.

PHILLACK (GWINEAR)

Little drops of water, little grains of sand,
Make the mighty ocean, and the pleasant land,
So the little minutes, humble as they be,
Make the mighty ages of Eternity.
(Julia Carney, 1823–1908: & also attributed to others)

The fates and fortunes of the folk of Phillack, with echoes of saints and sinners, ships and sheep and snails and spooky goings on, have been affected by the capricious nature of the sea and the shifting sands. Phillack, situated on a great bank of sand on the eastern side of the Hayle estuary, has its roots in antiquity, although much archaeological evidence now lies beneath the sand dunes. This was a busy and well populated area in times gone by, when traders with packhorses, sleighs and carts plied a network of ancient tracks converging on the Hayle estuary. Skeletons relating to those times have been discovered in the vicinity of Phillack churchtown. Hayle had emerged as an important port by 1799, and this gave rise to a regular passage of ships between here and Swansea. Several mine shafts were sunk in the Towans between Phillack and Gwithian, but the viability of the port of Hayle was always threatened by the build-up of sand in the estuary, made worse by the mining activity. Regular dredging was necessary to maintain a navigable channel for shipping. Over the centuries the encroachment of sand overwhelmed the town of Nikenor and several villages, but local folk endeavoured to turn a problem into an asset by selling the sand to farmers to use as fertiliser on their land.

From early times, sheep were traditionally driven to the Towans for the purpose of summer grazing, producing fine wool and meat with an agreeably distinctive flavour. A rare species of snail which had adapted to this windswept, salt-sprayed sandy habitat aroused great curiosity. Snails, like spiders, were thought to be prophetic, and if miners saw them on their way to work, they would proffer a crumb or other token of goodwill to guard against a mishap in the mine that day. Most people regarded them as lucky charms.

By the beginning of the 19th century, when the Riviere estate was in the possession of the Cornish Copper Company, the shifting sands had engulfed the fine castle of a formidable 6th-century chieftain called Theodore (or Teudor). In those days prevailing winds and currents had brought flotillas of Irish missionaries and their followers to these shores, much to the consternation of the local population. It soon became apparent that they came in peace, but as the zealous arrivals swarmed across the Hayle estuary and over Connor Downs, intent on preaching the good news and saving sinners, they were set upon and some were slain by Theodore. It was said that the missionary leader Fingar retreated to Gwinear with his head tucked under his arm, while other followers, suffering martyrdom at Theodore's

These dunes harbour a number of strange secrets.

hands, lent their names to Uny Lelant and Phillack. These massacres are recalled in the name of a 500-year-old inn, the Bucket of Blood.

The church of Phillack, which has managed to withstand the threatening sands and was largely rebuilt in 1856, retains a relic of these boisterous times. A stone slab in the gable of the porch bearing the monogram CHI RHO in a circle is supposedly the consecration stone of the first church. Four sons of the Hockin family achieved the remarkable distinction of serving as rectors here from 1763 to 1922. Canon Frederick, incumbent for 49 years, from 1853, had a small landing stage built to allow him to row across the pool to fetch supplies and visit his parishioners. The land-owning Hockin family also received dues from the mines worked on their property.

His father, William Hockin would have been the rector when a bizarre ritual was carried out in the churchyard at midnight in September 1844. Apparently a group of sick people who had engaged a scatterer of witch spells from Helston to cure them, paid the demanded fee and were brought here for an enactment of the removal of ill-wishing. The churchyard wall was sealed off and the participants were instructed to remain silent as the spell breaker prepared to perform his mysterious art. They watched in terror as he paced over the graves making strange noises and gesticulating, urging them to follow. Having encircled the church and trampled over the dead many times, it was reported that the doors and windows started to open and shut at his bidding. He commanded them to remain open, whereupon the images of those guilty of ill-wishing appeared to their victims, and thus the evil spells were broken and dissolved.

Somewhat eerily, a man called Erasmus Pascoe, who had defiled the holy well by washing his sheep in it, met a sequence of misfortunes, culminating in the death of his only son and, according to a tombstone of 1723, his own death two months later. Springs were always thought to be of sacred significance. The pagan Celts saw them as something to be worshipped, and the saints built on this tradition by making them holy wells.

While all this colourful activity must surely have left footprints in the sands of time, some strange occurrences more aptly recall a Shakespearian quotation from *The Tempest* regarding those who tread the sands 'with printless foot'. The area around Mexico Towans, the churchtown and the route into Hayle has long been the scene of psychic activity. In the 20th century, a number of late-night walkers heard the sound of approaching footsteps in Lethlean Lane, when no one was there. As the footsteps drew level, a sudden blast of cold air accompanied by a weird whooshing sound caused grown men to flee in terror. Dogs have also reacted to unseen forces in this area of psychic disturbance, becoming rooted to the spot, staring straight ahead, growling and being torn between fear and aggression.

Sightings of a ghost in a black cloak crossing the road from the rectory to the church, between the departure of one rector and the installation of the next, have been attributed to the long-serving, clerical Hockins, in pursuit of unfinished business. After the events of 1844, could this be William's way of ensuring that those who lay in the churchyard might rest in peace?

When troublesome spirits haunted buildings in days of yore, some exorcists attempted to contain the problem by imprisoning them in permanently locked rooms. Lanyon House in nearby Gwinear once had a chamber sealed for this purpose. Gwinear, which derived its name from one of the saints who was martyred by Theodore, had several haunted footpaths. In the early 19th century the body of a waggoner, who had apparently been run over by the wheel of his own cart, was discovered at the junction of a lane and a footpath leading to the local mine. Shortly after his body was removed, one of his old mates was accompanied by his phantom form as he walked along the track, uttering profanities he could not bring himself to repeat. This supernatural experience so traumatised the miner that he himself sickened and died soon afterwards.

Around that time, Elizabeth Thomas of Gwinear, who had been jilted by her lover, hanged herself from a tree adjoining a footpath along which she knew he would pass with his new fiancée. A prayer book found at her feet was seen open at the 'Cursing Psalm' (109), beside which she had written, 'When this you see, remember me'. She returned to haunt him for the rest of his life, and women shunned him for fear of being implicated in the spell. When he eventually found a widow willing to wed him, a localised tempest erupted above St Hilary's church, whereupon the ghost of his former sweetheart appeared menacingly on the path before them, with her open book. The service went ahead, but he was so exhausted in mind and body that all too soon he was laid to rest in the same churchyard.

PORTREATH

The place we now know as Portreath, and once called Basset's Cove, has experienced many natural and man-made changes over the centuries. Rising sea levels covered the wooded banks of the stream up the steep-sided valley, leaving a submerged forest, which is just visible offshore at exceptional states of the tide. The area now occupied by the village became swampy and silted up with sand, before the land stabilised. Its subsequent metamorphosis has been artificially induced.

The first anchorage for vessels was on the south side of the cove but, when mining was booming in the hinterland, a tramway and harbour were

Deadman's Hut at Portreath.

ingeniously created to export the copper ore to Swansea for smelting. Vessels returned with coal, which was stored at the harbourside. A guidebook of 1865 describes Portreath as 'a picturesque little place', while another published 35 years later said that 'it would be a picturesque little spot' were it not for 'the collection of coal yards in its midst'.

This once proud little port on the Atlantic seaboard, set in a narrow valley with towering hills and sombre cliffs, has an indefinable atmosphere of its own, and can be a bit oppressive to some. It has known the cruel sound of timbers crashing on the rocks and the anguished cries of drowning sailors above the raging storm. When shipwrecks occurred, survivors were taken to the Basset Arms, Smugglers' Cottage and other establishments to be looked after, while the corpses would be laid out in the mortuary on the site of the present Waterfront Inn, the old Pilots Hut, still known as Deadman's Hut, or in outbuildings of the Basset Arms. The seaborne hazards of this brutal coastline are reflected in names like Deadman's Cove and Hell's Mouth, while Ralph's Cupboard recalls the legendary giant Wrath, who preyed on fishermen in distress and added them to his menu. The name came to be associated with a daring smuggler called Ralph, whose expert seamanship allowed him to bring contraband goods ashore here.

Smugglers' Cottage on the south-west side of the cove, once used as a retreat by the enterprising Basset family of Tehidy who developed the harbour to serve the local mines, was associated with the moonshine brigade and supernatural happenings. An underground tunnel once linked it to a rock pool where the young Basset ladies used to bathe. It later became a popular guest house. During the course of alterations many years ago, a small secret closet was said to have been discovered which unaccountably contained the skeleton of a man seated at a small table wearing the remains of a black cloak, along with an ancient sea chest and a sword.

This old cottage adjoining the beach amongst the tamarisks was thought to be haunted by an apparition in the striking attire of an earlier era, which might be associated with the stylish blue uniforms trimmed with red and gold worn by the Portreath Artillery Volunteers. These were set up by Sir Francis Basset to man the cliff-top batteries and protect the coast from the threat of French and Spanish invasion. There would be a sudden drop in temperature as the ghostly figure emerged from a wooden panel by the blocked-off entrance to the old tunnel in a corridor on the first floor, before wafting towards the stairs, then vanishing. There were a number of sightings over many years, with dogs sometimes reacting to an unseen presence. A new structure has recently been erected on the site of Smugglers' Cottage, leaving very little of the original fabric.

The old port, which has been the scene of heroic endeavour and tragedy, has changed drastically over the last 30 years or so, with many of the fishermen's cottages and industrial structures around the harbour being replaced by more mundane development. Some associate this disturbance with a number of restless spirits in the vicinity, while Deadman's Hut above the dangerous harbour entrance strikes a chilling note.

Successive landlords of the Basset Arms, situated at the head of the cove, have seen shadowy figures in the bedroom upstairs and have attributed the mysterious movement of objects around the kitchen area to mischievous spooks. Staff and customers at the Portreath Arms Hotel have had eerie experiences after refurbishments were carried out. They speak of a 'presence', a cold touch on the shoulder and fleeting glimpses of a ghostly figure passing through the wall of the lounge bar, where a doorway has been blocked up. There has also been talk of a female apparition and unexplained incidents in the ladies' room, off the lounge bar.

Ghostly manifestations have also followed refurbishments at the Waterfront Inn, part of which incorporated the old mortuary. There have been claimed sightings of a misty male form in old-fashioned clothes. In the 1970s a lady diner caught sight of him and was so shocked at being able to see straight through him that she abandoned her meal and left. In the mid 1980s some workmen were surprised to see a ghostly figure in the doorway, which remained there for several minutes before vanishing. There have also been on-going sightings of phantom forms in the kitchen, with staff feeling that they were not alone. Soon after the Tregears took over in 2005, Helen Tregear caught sight of a male figure in a blue shirt, which she took to be her husband returning home earlier than expected. But it vanished without trace. Then the cook made mention of seeing someone in a blue shirt, who inexplicably disappeared. Helen said she sometimes had a feeling that someone was watching over her shoulder. It sent a shiver up her spine at first, but she adopted a philosophical attitude towards it, and said she only wished it would give a hand with the ironing and cleaning!

NANCEKUKE COMMON
(PORTHTOWAN)

In the 19th century, there was a gunpowder factory on Nancekuke Common on the exposed cliff-top plateau above Portreath, where a number of people lost their lives. When catastrophes occurred, the explosions could be heard for many miles around. This site was requisitioned for an airfield in July 1940, and the RAF station became operational the following March. There were four tarmac runways with Spitfires, Blenheims, Lysanders, Mosquitos, Halifaxes and Horsa gliders featuring among the aircraft operating from here.

Portreath started off as a fighter station, then assumed the role of a major ferry transport terminal for the RAF and the USAAF, with a number of squadrons from other areas coming here before setting out on missions to the Middle East, North Africa and other war zones. By the latter part of 1943 Portreath had resumed an offensive role, with Coastal Command's anti-shipping strike aircraft. The base was bombed by the Germans, and some of the young airmen lost their lives in accidents after take-off, but considering the difficult conditions, with inexperienced crews operating overweight aircraft, such losses were surprisingly light.

Young Jean Kane of Portreath (who later married one of the RAF personnel stationed there and ran the Choughs at Treswithian), recalls seeing two returning planes doing triumphant victory rolls, when they collided and crashed. Farmer Dick Eddy (see Treswithian) was on the cliff at Tehidy when he saw a plane crash on take-off, and remarked many years later, 'but we never heard anything about it'. To visit the immaculately kept RAF section of the churchyard at Illogan, where some of these brave young men are buried, is a very moving experience.

Flying operations were wound down at Portreath in 1945, with the station being reduced to Care and Maintenance that December. Between 1945 and 1950, Portreath housed a Transport Command Briefing School, and from 1946 to 1948 the outbuildings were used as a haven for the Polish Resettlement Air Corps.

In May 1950 the site was taken over by the Ministry of Supply as a Chemical Defence Establishment under the name of Nancekuke. The nerve agent Sarin was manufactured here, and later on chemicals and agents to support the UK's defensive research directed by Porton Down in Wiltshire. After the decision to decommission CDE Nancekuke in 1976, the site was taken over by the Ministry of Defence as a GCI Radar Station, and was formally re-opened as RAF Portreath on 1st October 1980. Today, the only active runway is used by Royal Air Force and Royal Navy helicopters.

There have long been reports of paranormal happenings associated with the airbase. Shortly after the Second World War, a young man who was working there moved with his family to a rented bungalow overlooking the sea at neighbouring Porthtowan. They became increasingly aware of the sound of footsteps and of doors opening and closing in empty rooms. This developed into hazy, then increasingly substantial sightings of a figure of a man in a blue RAF uniform sitting in an old rocking chair by the window, gazing contentedly out to sea, smoking his pipe. The phantom evaporated whenever anyone spoke to it and the chair stopped rocking.

After several weeks a local medium and her circle were brought in and, during a series of sessions, they contacted the spirit purported to be Flying Officer Peter Benson, who died after getting into difficulties during take-off with a Lockheed Hudson. The plane crashed near Mount Hawke.

A radar technician, carrying out a routine security check around the perimeter track in the mid-1980s, came across a situation he hadn't bargained for. He saw a figure in a Polish pilot's uniform approach the entrance to a hangar, then pass straight through the closed door. He returned to his colleagues white-faced and shaken. It turned out that they were well aware of this ghostly presence in their midst and had assumed a pragmatic attitude towards it. He was thought to be the pilot who crashed at nearby Bridge during the war.

People living down in the valley at Bridge, where WAAFs were billeted in Nissen huts which still exist, have spoken of several shadowy figures and a ghostly airman at the end of a building constructed after the war. One young man living in an outhouse sometimes experiences a very disconcerting feeling of being watched through the window, and his family have often felt the presence of their forebears and their pets, who took up residence here shortly after the Second World War.

PRAA SANDS

The far famed ruined castle at Praa Sands on the shores of Mount's Bay, was cited as the most haunted location in the UK by the prestigious Ghost Club Society in January 2001. Over the centuries, fragments of half-remembered history are embellished in the telling and retelling, becoming increasingly weird and mystical. Some people believed that the castle had been raised in three nights, and was destined to vanish in spectacular style.

According to tradition, Pengersick castle was built in the reign of Henry VIII, by a merchant who had acquired such enormous wealth beyond the seas that it

The ruined castle of Pengersick.

broke the back of an ass as it was being loaded on the shore. Towards the end of that monarch's reign the place was reputedly acquired by one of the Milliton family, who had slaughtered a man on the streets of London during a drunken brawl, and secluded himself in a private chamber in the tower for the rest of his life.

The old man, who was keen to forge links with leading Cornish families, wanted his son to marry an elderly heiress who was infatuated with him. But when the lady realised that her amorous advances and love potions concocted by the Witch of Fraddam were to no avail, she decided to marry his father as a means of getting revenge on the one who had spurned her. Having convinced her husband that she had been raped by her stepson, and was carrying his child, the pair hatched a plot for him to be sold into slavery, but he fled overseas before the bandits arrived to carry him off. When the young Lord of Pengersick returned a few years later with a beautiful Eastern princess in tow, he discovered that his scheming stepmother had become disfigured on account of meddling with poisons in an attempt to do away with his father and seize his worldly goods.

Local folk never knew what went on behind those castle walls, but it was rumoured that having become acquainted with the mystical arts of the East, Lord Pengersick was obsessed with magical spells, making experiments which produced noxious smoke and raising spirits by weird incantations. If the couple's sudden arrival had caused a stir, their departure on a dark and stormy night was rather more spectacular. For a sudden glow in the sky seen from miles around, gave way to catastrophic splendour as flames engulfed the castle, and the forms of Lord Pengersick, his dusky lady and a mysterious visitor were catapulted into Eternity in a searing blaze of light.

Owner, Angela Evans, in the haunted bedroom at Pengersick castle.

A more conventional approach to the history of Pengersick would indicate that the early inhabitants of Mount's Bay gleaned a livelihood from the bounty of the sea, the cultivation of the land and the exploitation of tin. Seaborne trade was probably carried on by flat-bottomed vessels, capable of landing on the beach, and small-scale fishing activity supplemented by smuggling and wrecking. The shores of Mount's Bay had always been vulnerable to seafaring marauders and, when the Pengersick family came to the fore in the 13th century, having acquired wealth and power, they constructed a fine defended manor house to the north-east of the present castle.

According to the records, one Richard de Pengersick was murdered in 1221. The first Henry Pengersick, who died in 1327, married a member of the Godolphin family, and their son Henry found himself in trouble three years later for grievously wounding the vicar of Breage. The Pengersick estate received a welcome boost when his granddaughter married John Bevill, and they had a chapel built there.

The place fell into decline when Isabell Bevill married Thomas Worth and moved to Devon, but when the estate subsequently passed to her daughter Elizabeth, wife of John Milliton of Meavy, they decided to construct a larger and grander castellated mansion with two courtyards. Most of the bizarre legends were attached to the Millitons, who may have been regarded as foreign upstarts and treated with suspicion by the locals and, as time went on, their antics merged with those of their forebears. The Millitons went on to play an influential role in the life of the county. Their son John became Captain of St Michael's Mount in 1522 and both he and his son William were Sheriffs of Cornwall.

William Milliton and his wife Honor, who had seven daughters and then a son, thought they had secured an heir at last, but sadly he died in tragic circumstances whilst travelling overseas. The fates and fortunes of Pengersick took a nose dive when the inheritance was split between the surviving daughters and all too soon it degenerated into a romantic ruin.

It would seem that the thick granite walls of the remaining tower hold many secrets. Experts in the paranormal field have evidence of psychic and poltergeist activity. They have spoken of darting lights, known as orbs, eerie echoes in the tower, a black hound with blazing red eyes, shadowy rats with long tails rushing round the garden, ascending white vapours which sometimes develop into ghostly female forms, and even a shocking re-enactment of a rape and two murders. Seasoned ghost hunters claim to have made contact with 20 or so presences, including ghostly monks in the tower and in the garden, sometimes heard chanting; a phantom knight taken to be Henry Le Fort or John Milliton; and two female apparitions. One of these is cited as Engreine, wife of the first Henry Pengersick. A medium using a pendant declared that she had been in touch with William Milliton, who had practised alchemy there. No one has been able to identify the little girl in red who danced over the top of the highest turret, and tried to lure others toward the top of the tower. Alexander, the masterful castle cat, who takes an enthusiastic part in organised paranormal investigations, reacts to some manifestations and was clearly bemused when he failed to capture any of the darting phantom rodents.

Alexander, the castle cat, who attempted to capture phantom rodents.

There are times when the well-prepared sophisticated equipment used by teams of experienced investigators inexplicably breaks down. However, the most positive results seem to be centred on the third floor bedroom, where a monk, a knight, two ladies in 13th-century apparel and a demon hound have put in appearances. Most memorable was a tall, slim lady with an aristocratic air seen emerging from the bedroom wall who seemed to be searching for something. She wore a full length pale coloured gown, with a sparkling jewel hanging from the front of an ornate belt.

One of the most dramatic sightings occurred when a misty white vapour, arising from the four-poster bed, took on the form of a woman wearing a long sleeved nightgown, patterned below the neckline. She emerged from the bed clutching her abdomen as though in pain, then lay down again. At this point another female apparition wafted through the wall, clad in an unevenly textured black, three-quarter length coat over a shiny cream-coloured dress. She glided around as if ministering to the prone ghostly figure on the bed.

ST MICHAEL'S MOUNT

St Michael's Mount, rising majestically above the capricious waters of Mount's Bay, possesses an ethereal, haunting quality all of its own. It is a magical place where primeval, pagan and Christian forces combine with whimsical Celtic myths and legends. The conical formation was formerly known as 'the hoare rock in the wood', and sections of a subterranean forest exposed at low tide reveal where the elk, the wolf and the boar once roamed and, even earlier, the bear, the lion and the mastodon.

According to legend, the Mount was the domain of the giant Cormoran, whose wife was accidentally killed when she got in the way of a cobbling hammer being thrown by the friendly giant Trecobben, who in turn died of grief. Cormoran, who had the annoying habit of wading ashore and snatching folks' sheep and cows, met his end after an artful local lad called Jack rowed out as he slept, dug a pit in the hillside and blew on his horn. When the angry giant came rushing down the slope, he fell headlong into the pit; whereupon brave Jack received a reward and became immortalised as Jack, the Giant Killer. Successive generations believed the place to be haunted by an exceptionally tall man.

Strangely, during renovation work about 160 years ago, a low Gothic doorway was discovered in

The dramatic history of St Michael's Mount is reflected in paranormal activity today.

the south wall of the chapel on the Mount, which had been closed by masonry and concealed by a platform. Further investigation revealed a flight of steps leading to a small chamber, where the bones of a 7ft 8in man were discovered, with no sign of a coffin.

The anchorage between Marazion and the famous Mount was once the busy scene of prehistoric trading activity. Some people believe this rocky little islet to have been the Ictis of ancient times, where the Phoenicians came in quest of tin, thereby conjuring up romantic visions of handsome craft with billowing silken sails. They were said to have established the worship of Apollo here, attracting pilgrims with innumerable offerings, and the tradition continued with the monastic foundation. The sacred site became even more significant after some humble fishermen claimed to have seen a vision of the Archangel St Michael on a rocky ledge high above the sea on the western side.

There was a Celtic monastery on the summit of the Mount long before Edward the Confessor gave it to the Benedictine Abbey of Mont St Michel in Normandy. The monastic church was destroyed by an earthquake in 1275, and the Black Death left the Prior with only two of his twelve monks. The present church dates from the 14th century. Although the place has an aura of peace and tranquillity, it has been the scene of many brutal happenings over the centuries, which led to it becoming a 'fortalice to all the country round', as well as a monastery.

St Michael's Mount has borne witness to a catalogue of suffering, strife, and painful human experience, in pursuit of godliness and power. Some who had sought refuge here were brutalised when the place was captured, and prisoners of state were also held here. The Mount has been involved in military sieges on several occasions, sometimes employing the old strategy of soldiers gaining entry disguised as pilgrims, causing some surprise as they flourished the weapons they concealed beneath their garments. Perkin Warbeck's wife took refuge here during the Rebellion of 1497, and the castle was taken by storm during Flamank's rebellion. It was taken and plundered by Arundel's rebels during the reign of Edward VI, and was held by the Royalists during the Civil War. Col St Aubyn was nominated Captain of the Mount in 1647. The St Aubyn family purchased the Mount twelve years later, and it remains their home today. The 18th-century antiquary William Borlase put the history of St Michael's Mount in a nutshell, saying, 'Anciently only a monastery, in tumultuous and warlike times a fort and monastery together, since the Reformation a fort only, and now neither a fort nor monastery, but a neat comfortable and secure dwelling house.'

The dramatic things that occurred here over the centuries have given rise to reports of supernatural happenings. These include a ghostly figure in a monk's habit, which seems confused and lost. It has been suggested that he might be looking for the monastery destroyed by the earthquake and replaced by a church a couple of hundred years later.

One of the National Trust's head guides, who had worked on the Mount for many years, said that he had once got a glimpse of a male apparition wearing a blue frock coat and knee breeches sitting at the end of a passageway. A lady in grey, said to have been a lady-in-waiting and nanny to the St Aubyn family in the 1750s, has also been seen several times. She threw herself from the rooftop when she discovered that the man who had made her pregnant refused to stand by her. Despite her tragic end, she is regarded as a friendly ghost.

A 17th-century four-poster bedstead in which many people must have slept reputedly radiates a strange atmosphere. The story goes that no child has been able to pass the night in this bed and some visitors have an uneasy feeling of not being alone as they enter this room.

TOWEDNACK

The parish of Towednack, about three miles to the south-west of St Ives, lies in an exposed and elevated granitic mining district, rich in archaeological remains and colourful folklore, where the whimsical spills over into the supernatural. This area is famous for the discovery of a late Bronze Age golden treasure; its distinctive squat church and Feast Day customs; and the Wise Men of Towednack who tried to build a hedge around a cuckoo in an attempt to preserve eternal spring. This may or may not have influenced local tradition whereby anyone making an absurd utterance was told to go to Towednack quay where they christen calves (no part of the parish actually adjoined the coastline). The logical cure for colic in Towednack was to stand on one's head for half an hour. Alongside all this flippancy, the miners and agricultural workers who lived here had an awareness of the past and an affinity with this mysterious landscape.

In ancient times, important people like tribal leaders were laid to rest in the conspicuously-sited burial mounds that we see today, along with treasured artefacts for their enjoyment in the afterlife, as discovered at Amalveor. Some say that the custom died out as they became more spiritual, and there is a school of thought that subsequent cremations may have been made in an attempt to dispose of the dead and their ghosts. Be that as it may, there have long been reports of weird happenings and ghostly goings-on in this wild and craggy moorland area.

According to legend, the construction of Towednack's church tower was hampered by the devil's antics.

There was an age-old tradition that the tower of the pleasing little church which blends in so well with its rugged environment, without buttresses or pinnacles, was never completed on account of the devil destroying by night the painstaking work carried out by the builders during the day. On feast days the parishioners were met at the church door by a fiddler or 'crowder', who led them in procession, singing and dancing through the lanes, banishing the forces of darkness.

Many years ago, a mine carpenter called John Martin, who dwelt at Embla, was haunted by the spirit of an old acquaintance, whose coffin he had made. The villagers were puzzled why this fine figure of a man was suddenly becoming a physical wreck. Then one day a young man from the village, who had fallen out with his family, called on Mr John to ask if he could stay with him. As the carpenter was just off for the night shift, he said that the lad could sleep in his bed, adding that if he experienced strange noises in the night, he was not to worry.

That night the young man suddenly awoke, with a feeling that a visitor had entered the cottage through the front door. Then he heard the sound of someone climbing the stairs. Feeling very uneasy he called out, 'Hello! Who's there?' but there was no reply. He got up and went to investigate, but there was nobody there. So he bolted the door, returned to bed and tossed and turned for the rest of the night.

When Mr John returned the next morning he was not surprised to hear what had happened, and confessed that he had long been troubled by eerie experiences like this. He said that he had kept quiet about it, fearing that folk might laugh at him. Nothing would induce the lad to stay any longer, and through him the villagers became aware of what was troubling poor Mr John.

The hauntings got steadily worse after this until it reached the point that the presence followed him wherever he went, then began to manifest itself as an apparition. Eventually he made up his mind to speak to the ghost when it made its next appearance, and this happened one night as he was passing Towednack church. There standing in front of him, against a hedge, was the spectre and, plucking up his courage, Mr John confronted it, saying, 'In the name of God, what do you want?' It replied, 'I'm glad you have spoken to me; I have waited long for you to do so.' There followed a conversation, the nature of which was never to be disclosed to any living person. The carpenter was given to understand that the spirit would never trouble him again if he kept his secret. From that moment Mr John started to regain his health and lived to a ripe old age.

The mine workings in this

The mines were thought to be haunted by little sprites, known as knockers, or buccas.

area are thought to be the most ancient in Cornwall, and subsequent miners who broke into old shafts and adits came across stags' horns, pickaxes and other early implements. Some maintained that it was possible to hear these ghostly miners at work, with the sounds of pickaxes, the rolling of barrows and falling earth and stones and eerie voices at night, when labour had ceased. Early arrivals at work claim to have glimpsed the little sprites caught unawares, sitting on timbers or frolicking around. There was a long-held belief that these spirits, also known as knockers or buccas, haunted the mines, having supposedly perished in mining accidents. They could be mischievous, or helpful and protective towards the miners in their dangerous daily toil, if they were treated with respect.

A rather lazy Towednack miner called Barker, who scoffed at the suggestion that these little imps suspended between heaven and hell had powers for good or evil, experienced an eerie comeuppance for such scepticism. He went to spy on them and overheard them discussing where to hide their tools. One said he would leave them in a cleft in the rock, and another that he would put them under the ferns. The third one declared, 'I shall leave mine on Barker's knee!' And at that moment Barker felt a terrific blow on his knee, with his screams being drowned by the gleeful laughter echoing from the mineshaft. The poor

The dramatic landscape has long been associated with supernatural happenings.

man walked with a limp for the rest of his life, but found an enduring place in local parlance, where 'As stiff as Barker's knee' became a common saying.

Who knows what supernatural force led Henry Berryman, another miner from Towednack, to a rich seam of tin in this locality when he was far away from home? Having emigrated to California he dreamt that he was working for tin in a rich cross course lode in a nearby mine in Nancledra, and went to investigate this on his return, to no avail. When he was in Montana some years later he had the same dream, and again during the journey home. On his arrival he employed a dowser whose dowsing rods pinpointed a particular spot. These rods continued to demonstrate the exact alignment of the mineral wealth which lurked beneath the surface, as the dowser moved around, blindfolded.

This mysterious landscape, with its fantastically weathered granite boulders, old mine workings and the tombs and temples of our ancient ancestors strewn across the high and wild terrain, has long been associated with the King of the Giants, witches and fairies. Witches Rock, between Nancledra Bottoms and Zennor is where the Witches of Penwith traditionally gathered on Midsummer Eve to renew their vows and revive their supernatural powers, lighting fires in rock basins and on cromlechs, until the hillsides were alive with flames. Although it was said that the witches fled when their rock was removed, their supernatural legacy lingers on.

CRAFTHOLE

The Finnygook Inn was once a hive of smuggling activity.

The hamlet of Crafthole, in the parish of Sheviock, situated between the Lynher River and Whitsand Bay, has experienced a vibrant and colourful past, with fluctuating fates and fortunes. Long-established traditions of hospitality are continued at the old Finnygook Inn, where at least one ghostly character still makes its presence felt, prompting speculation about who he might have been.

In the old days Crafthole was an important resting point for weary travellers on the much-frequented highway between the Cremyll ferry and Liskeard. At one time it was a borough, governed by a port reeve, assisted by two constables, and folk from far and wide thronging the twice-weekly markets and annual fair came here to whet their whistles. The 17th-century inhabitants of Crafthole had a far flung reputation for cohabiting with other people's spouses, and travellers, wont to chaff them about their loose morals, needed to be fleet of foot when the women retaliated with their ever ready buckets of stinking slops. These impoverished families lived by labouring on the land or fishing down at Portwrinkle, and many would have been heavily involved in the notorious smuggling activities in Whitsand Bay. Ghostly encounters are still being reported in the steep lane up from Portwrinkle, on the old smuggling route inland, now known as Finnygook Lane, and people walking down the lane at twilight speak of an apparently normal person coming towards them and suddenly vanishing. Some had wished him a cheery 'Goodnight' and wondered why they got no response; while many others steadfastly avoid the lane they believe to be haunted at dusk.

Smuggling had long been an accepted way of life here, for Whitsand Bay with its wide expanse of sand and thickly vegetated rocky cliff line was an ideal place for landing cargoes, while high-hedged fields and lanes offered favourable opportunities of running the goods inland without too much interference from the riding officers or customs men. Sampling the contents of one of the kegs, however, was the undoing of one of the local fraternity from Downderry, who was captured drunk and incapable in the aptly named Grog Lane. Fishing boats from the little harbour at Portwrinkle were involved in the trade, and Smuggler's Cottage, built by Thomas Helman in 1795, bears witness to the jolly heyday of 'free trading'. It had a secret compartment beneath some flagstones, which could accommodate a couple of kegs. Eventually a coastguard station was established here.

The area saw many skirmishes between the searchers and free traders, although some in authority may have worn 'fog spectacles with bank note shades'. They offered tempting rewards for information leading to the arrest of smugglers, but betraying the fraternity was an unpardonable sin, usually resulting in long drawn out, brutal retribution.

According to local tradition an 18th-century smuggler called Silas Finny had a disagreement with his associates over the handling of a consignment of brandy, lace and tobacco due to be landed in Whitsand Bay. In a fit of pique he revealed their plans to the authorities, and made himself scarce when they were captured red-handed in the midst of unloading the illicit cargo on the sands in the moonlight. They were deported to Botany Bay, but things came home to roost for their informer many years later, when he was foully done to death at Bligers Well, halfway up the hill between Portwrinkle and Crafthole. Since that time the ghost of Finny (or Finnygook) has reputedly haunted the lane and the former New Inn was renamed in honour of the once regular drinker who paid the ultimate price for his betrayal and who seems reluctant to leave.

FALMOUTH

The capacious estuary of the Fal has been the busy scene of maritime activity since early times. Some historians believe that the Phoenicians came here in quest of tin long before the Greek and Roman traders arrived on the scene. Oyster-dredging has been carried out in the river since Roman times, and the tradition continues today, using methods which have changed very little. A few years ago a local fisherman engaged in oyster-dredging in the Carrick Roads was astonished to see a graceful fleet of vessels entering the haven under full sail, creating a vibrant spectacle which gradually faded away. Although he was excitedly pointing out details, his colleague seemed unable to see it.

It was Sir Walter Raleigh who first recognised the full potential of this deep water anchorage and urged the development of a township close to the mouth of the haven, on the western side. The land-owning Killigrews pressed ahead with the scheme, establishing a focal centre for the ever-growing number of ships and seafarers who called here. Later on, the Killigrews remained loyal to the king during the Civil War, and Falmouth received a Charter.

The Church of King Charles the Martyr is a reminder of the impact of the Civil War on Falmouth. There have been reports of sightings of phantom

The entrance to Falmouth harbour.

figures relating to that period of time in various parts of the town, and in the vicinity of the churchyard.

A family moving into a three-storey house with a basement in Penwerris Terrace, overlooking the Penryn River, saw an image of a Cavalier reflected in a mirror they were positioning on a wall. In Bar Terrace a Cavalier was also seen, entering the front door of one of the houses, proceeding through the rear garden and wafting along the railway line in the direction of the castle.

This area had always been vulnerable to attack by sea, and cannon balls recovered from the riverbed from time to time recall past skirmishes with French and Spanish vessels, extending almost to Truro on one occasion. There had been a fort on the headland of Pendennis long before Henry VIII established a castle here on land owned by the Killigrews, as one of a string of fortresses along this southern coast. Thankfully, the feared invasions by the French and Spanish never materialised. As it transpired, the liveliest time at the castle was not on account of attack by foreigners, but hostility from fellow countrymen during the aforementioned Civil War. Pendennis famously stood out for a five-month siege by land and sea under the brave 70-year-old commander, Sir John Arundell.

During the siege there was enormous hardship, with the defenders of the fortress reduced to eating horse and dog meat. They also suffered from the plague. When they were eventually forced to capitulate, their stout-hearted commander was able to organise an honourable retreat, marching through the castle gate with flying colours, trumpets sounding and drums beating. Thus they made a glorious departure, leaving behind them 200 sick and about the same number of women and children. Some would say that many of the victims remain, in ghostly form. The sound of horses' hooves has even been heard in the vicinity of Horsepool Bastion.

Pendennis Castle is considered a 'hot spot' by paranormal investigators.

The history of Pendennis Castle encompasses many great historical events from the Spanish Armada to the Napoleonic conflicts and the two World Wars, when the headland's coastal defences and searchlight installations below, guarded Falmouth Docks from enemy attack. There has been a succession of structural changes in that time, with gatehouses, guardrooms, barracks, stores, houses, gun batteries and observation posts being erected. The port was taken over by the Admiralty in times of strife, and the 105th Regiment of Royal Garrison Artillery moved to Pendennis after the modernisation of Falmouth's defences at the turn of the 19th century. They and the Miners Militia, who were the forerunners of the Territorial Army and also based here, held regular practice exercises.

In the 20th century Pendennis and St Mawes castles became the command centre for the defences of the whole of south-west Cornwall, the western approaches and the strategic entrance to the English Channel. Falmouth became a training camp and port of departure for new recruits before they were dispatched to the trenches in France in the First World War, and the castle served as an officers' mess. Nissen huts were built within the castle complex and on Hornwork Common to accommodate an ever-changing succession of soldiers in the Second World War. The castle became the headquarters of the Commander Fixed Defences Falmouth, and again the officers' mess. There was a great deal of secret activity going on in the Fal and Helford rivers, and in the build-up to the raid on St Nazaire and the D-Day landings. Some of the paranormal happenings at the castle relate to these comparatively recent times.

Paranormal experts with their hi-tech equipment regard Pendennis Castle as a hotspot, with the profusion of spirit globes creating a veritable 'light show' during their nocturnal investigations. Many of the ghostly forms are thought to emanate from the famous siege during the Civil War when hundreds of people, including women and children died here. A childish figure in Civil War attire has been seen making his way up the spiral staircase in the Tudor kitchen and several members of staff have reported sightings of a ghostly female disappearing up some now blocked up stairs.

The figure of another lady, who emerges from a possible gravesite and walks diagonally across the lawned area before disappearing into thin air, is believed to be the wife of one of the Royalist officers. Visitors have spoken of a female apparition of indeterminate age who traverses the site. When she was spotted by some workmen early one morning, before the staff arrived, they thought she was a member of the public who had sneaked in through an open gate. But as one of them went over to tell her that the castle was not yet open, he was shocked to realise that she was invisible below mid-calf level, before she simply vanished. It seems the site has undergone comprehensive alterations over the centuries, and she was apparently walking on a former, lower level.

As one of the custodians was locking up in the late afternoon in December 2004, after everyone had gone home, he heard the sound of children's laughter.

Looking towards the East Bastion he saw the upper part of the figure of a small child, with a shock of black hair, wearing a red top, pop up behind the wall. As he rushed over to investigate he realised that a sheer drop behind the wall made this impossible. He carried out a comprehensive search, but there was no child to be seen.

There have also been several sightings of a soldier who comes up through the floor of the guardhouse and proceeds round the corner before evaporating. He wears a khaki uniform of the type worn in the Second World War. Those working in the shop are also well aware of thumps and bumps, footsteps and other strange noises emanating from the area above. Some returning servicemen refuse to go up there today, on account of terrifying supernatural experiences while they were stationed there. This is where there have been sightings of another soldier with what appears to be bandages around his head and legs. It is known that this was once a military hospital, and he is thought to have been one of those who died here during the First World War.

LISKEARD

Braddock Downs, between Lostwithiel and Liskeard, was the scene of the first battle of the Civil War fought on Cornish soil. In Cornwall there was a period of manoeuvring for the allegiance of the towns and control of the militia, before the first clouds of war finally broke over the county. On this side of the Tamar it was a situation with strong religious, rather than political connotations, which divided families, friends and neighbours.

Ghostly screams and shouts heard on Braddock Downs recall the bloody battle there in 1643. (Sketch by Julia Draper)

As the Parliamentary forces gathered on the other side of the Tamar, an army of volunteers raised by the Royalist gentry of Cornwall and drawn mostly from their loyal servants and tenants, prepared themselves for action. The force consisted of only 1,500 foot soldiers with stout hearts, but few guns. The advanced guard of Parliamentarians led by the Scottish Colonel Ruthven had been repulsed when attempting to force a passage at Saltash, but when they succeeded in crossing the Tamar at Gunnislake, the Royalists retreated to Bodmin, where a great number of the militia had also assembled. The Royalist leader Sir Ralph Hopton knew that he must destroy Ruthven before he was backed up by the main body of Parliamentarians under the Earl of Stamford, who was marching with all haste from Launceston with a large force of men and horses.

On Wednesday 18th January 1643, the Royalists left Bodmin and spent the night under the hedges of Boconnoc Park, Lord Mohun's estate, where fires were lit. Meanwhile Ruthven, who had decided not to hang about for Stamford's reinforcements to arrive, advanced from Liskeard, and drew up his army on the downs in front of the little church at Braddock, only a couple of miles away from Boconnoc.

The Royalist Sir Bevil Grenville led the vanguard. After solemn prayers had been said at the head of each division, the infantry burst in on the enemy lines, while the cavalry charged them from the flank. Their fearless commander led his men in so fierce a charge that the enemy broke ranks and fled. It was a complete rout with the cavalry pursuing their enemy into Liskeard and beyond. In the course of this short but decisive battle, the Royalist losses were light. However, 200 Parliamentarian soldiers were slaughtered on this beautiful Cornish hillside and 1,200 were taken prisoner.

Since that time there have been reports of sounds of strife, with shouts, screams and the pounding of horses' hooves re-echoing across the terrain on the anniversary of the battle. There have also been claimed sightings of eerie fleeting figures associated with that day of triumph and tragedy.

LOOE ISLAND

Time was when the sound of chanting monks echoed across the narrow strip of water dividing Looe Island from the mainland. It came from an ancient chapel on the island's summit. Some fancy it may still be heard today. A second chapel was built on the mainland opposite to accommodate worshippers who didn't want to make the sometimes treacherous crossing. Looe Island is also associated with the legend about Jesus and his uncle Joseph of Arimathea visiting Cornwall in quest of tin. The alleged visit inspired the poet William Blake to pen the immortal lines:

And did those feet in ancient times,
Walk upon England's mountains green,
And was the holy Lamb of God
On England's pleasant pastures seen?

Although so close to the shore, the salt-sprayed island environment was effectively a little world of its own. The focus of life was always the sea, and it was the scene of smuggling, piratical and wrecking activities of a particularly rumbustious nature. Many vessels met their doom in these hazardous waters, and bodies of shipwrecked mariners were washed up on these shores from time to time.

Looe Island, variously known as St Michael's, St Nicholas' and St George's Island, which served as an outpost of Glastonbury Abbey, passed to the Crown in the 13th century. It was in the ownership of the Mayows (or Mays) in the 16th century, and was acquired by the Trelawnys of Trelawne in the mid-18th century. When left uninhabited, it became the domain of a variety of seabirds but various people did take up residence in the old buildings during the ownership of the Trelawnys, and they constructed a new house there in the 1870s.

Certain notoriety surrounded the Finns, who arrived on the scene around 1783 and were heavily involved in smuggling. They remained on the island for about 40 years. It seems that an outlaw named Finn (or Fynn), who had been banished to the Mewstone Rock off Plymouth Sound for a term of seven years, ventured westwards by sea and decided to settle here after serving his sentence. His family cultivated the land, kept two cows and a horse, and created secret chambers for the storage of contraband goods beneath the buildings, assisted by a black man. They were joined by the Hooper family, who collaborated closely with them in all their dealings.

The daring exploits of the local smugglers

There have long been reports of paranormal activity on Looe Island.

centred on Looe Island commanded admiration all along the coast. Tea, tobacco, brandy, silks and satins, as well as a host of other luxury goods found their way to the secret caves and cellars here, before being taken to the mainland and transported inland, under cover of darkness, through narrow lanes said to be haunted. Looe Island became so notorious that the authorities stationed preventive men here, but this did not cramp the perpetrators' style too much.

Over many decades there have been reports of paranormal activity on Looe Island, usually associated with a strange blue haze. Around 1850 William and Jane Vague were in residence and they invited a family friend, a young dressmaker, to stay while she carried out some tailoring work for them. Her visit coincided with the husband's overnight trip to the mainland on business. Their guest savoured her visit to the full by doing her sewing outdoors on a seat near the summit of the island. Feelings of peace and well-being soon gave way to a strange and uneasy sensation that some unseen person was lurking behind her. So she went back to the house and returned with one of the children to keep her company. However, the little girl soon became disturbed and restless and insisted on returning to her mother. She remained fractious for the rest of the day.

At about 9 o'clock the dressmaker retired to the bed she was to share with her hostess, the children asleep in a cot alongside. After sleeping peacefully for a few hours, she suddenly became wide awake for no apparent reason. She then became aware of a bluish light and the figure of a tall aristocratic-looking man with grey hair and elegant hands and particularly long fingers emerged from the wall. He crossed the room slowly in the midst of the haze and disappeared through the wall opposite. Although she was very frightened, the dressmaker crept out of bed at daybreak and went downstairs to check all was well. She found nothing amiss but could not bring herself to tell her hosts what she had seen, and left rather abruptly the next day.

Some years ago, a skeleton was unearthed near the seat where the seamstress had sat. It was that of a tall man with exceptionally long fingers but speculation remains as to his identity.

PENTEWAN – HELIGAN GARDENS

In the days when it was fashionable for the gentry to demonstrate their power and status by creating fine gardens, impressive drives sweeping up to front doors and prestigious symbols at outer entrances, it was said of the stone balls topping Heligan's gateposts:

When they stone balls see Squire Tremayne,
They jump to the ground, then they leap back again.

Local folk may have relished the rhyme with tongue in cheek, but as the years rolled on and worldwide events made an impact here, much spookier things began to happen in the gardens famed for some of the largest Himalayan rhododendrons in the kingdom and described as exquisite in the 19th century.

Heligan, first documented in the 12th century, is pleasingly situated at the head of a valley where springs abound, overlooking Mevagissey Bay. The name, signifying the profusion of willow trees which once flourished in this moist and humid atmosphere, has melancholy and romantic connotations beloved by poets and dreamers.

The Tremayne family, originally from Devon, acquired Heligan in the 16th century and built a mansion on the site of a former manor house in 1603. This was enlarged and upgraded later that century and in the early part of the 19th century. Various members of the family had demonstrated their worth on the battlefield, become lawyers and made prudent marriages, thus consolidating their position as one of Cornwall's foremost families. It was always the gardens, not the house, which were envied by the local gentry and admired by the public, who in the latter part of the 19th century were permitted to view them by arrangement. In its heyday the large estate was entirely self-supporting. It had farms, quarries, brickworks, woodlands and a saw mill, a grist mill and a brewery. The gardens had to be functional as well as beautiful, with orchards and vegetable gardens. It took a great deal of expertise for the gardeners to produce enough fruit and vegetables for the Tremaynes and their guests, as well as feeding a workforce of over 40, and their families.

At the beginning of the 19th century, inheriting Heligan came as a bit of a surprise to Henry Hawkins Tremayne, a curate in Lostwithiel, who was also bequeathed a family estate near Wadebridge, and a further one in Devonshire shortly afterwards. His fresh approach breathed new life into the gardens, however, and he commissioned Thomas Gray to draw up a plan and establish the basic pattern of the grounds we see today. His son, grandson and great grandson all became noted horticulturalists and built up the impressive collection of plants. It was John Heale Tremayne who created the splendid Long Drive, lined with ornamental trees and the magnificent avenue of *Cornus capitata*. His son John created the exotic Jungle, and he and his son John Claude introduced the palms, tree ferns and bamboos which became such a feature of the gardens.

Unfortunately, the First World War robbed Heligan of its enthusiastic young workforce, many of whom were destined to die on the fields of Flanders, so far removed from this idyllic environment. Things could never be the same again. Heligan House became a convalescent home for officers during the First World War, and American officers were billeted here during rehearsals for the D-Day landings during the Second World War. The house was subsequently let to tenants before being converted and sold off as flats in the 1970s. Meanwhile the gardens had been neglected, and the more rampant of the introduced plants had taken over. The artificial environment of a garden was aptly described by Tim Smit, who was instrumental in its restoration, as a 'symbol of man's arrogance, perverting nature to human ends'.

There have long been reports of a ghostly grey lady, regularly spotted walking away from the house down a path shown on old maps as Grey Lady's Walk, before disappearing into the trees. In more recent times, residents of Heligan House noticed doors opening and closing for no apparent reason and eerie echoing footsteps, leading to speculation as to whether the Tremaynes and their well-heeled guests had returned to their former home.

It was reckoned that a number of ghosts were disturbed when the gardens were being restored to their former glory. There were general feelings of not being alone, and of hearing footsteps when no one was around. Staff found items from locked rooms turning up elsewhere and there were times when the inexplicable opening and closing of seeding pot lids in sequence, ended with a gentle sigh. Several people have spoken of strange goings on in the Crystal Grotto, where a ghostly form moved across the ground and vanished through the wall. Psychics mentioned a tragic couple who used to meet there in secret, while some asserted that there were 'dark humours abroad' in the grounds. In his book *The Lost Gardens of Heligan*, Tim Smit described some of the more sinister happenings which led to certain areas of the garden being exorcised by the local vicar, thereby lifting the atmosphere of haunting sadness.

PERRANWELL STATION

Perranwell lies in the heart of an old mining and agricultural district, where the September Moggy Fair was the highlight of the year. Cattle, horses and other livestock were bought and sold at the fair, peddlers and traders plied their wares, local folk indulged in sports and games, and all the inns laid on tempting fare. The establishment of the branch line from Truro to Falmouth in 1863 brought more people here and focused attention on the place now known as Perranwell Station. The colourful fair has long gone, but the tradition of animal husbandry lives on, in an area which provides ideal meadows and paddocks for keeping horses, and offers the opportunity of riding in quiet country lanes and off the roads.

Paul, a farrier, occupies a property whose 19th-century farmhouse burnt down and was never rebuilt. He lives in the old cob-built cowman's cottage, which was extended in the 1940s. He moved in with his mother in 1971 and brought up his own family there. Paul has been a horseman all his life and, as well as looking after his own and his neighbours' horses, the family has a reputation for showing compassion towards horses which have been ill-treated. It seems that some of the horses who have passed on over the years have been reluctant to leave the place where they were treated so kindly.

Paul's wife, Karen, got a shock a few years ago, when a friend who had not visited before made a comment about the solitary little horse in one of the fields, with banana-shaped legs. She went on to give a detailed description of Nipper, a strong-willed little bay pony with bowlegs, which had been in livery at the farm, but which had died two years earlier. When they went out to investigate, the field was empty.

Some time later, Paul's son was returning home one moonlit night when he heard the sound of galloping hooves coming up behind him. It got closer and

One of the haunted fields at Perranwell Station.

closer, but when he looked over his shoulder the lane was quite empty. When the frightened lad reached home, white and trembling, Paul was convinced that this was the ghost of Millie, a breeding horse which had recently had to be put down. A number of other people have had a similar experience in the lane since then.

When the house was being renovated, Paul and his wife were living in a caravan in the farmyard. They were disturbed one night by the sound of galloping in one of the top fields. They went out to have a look, but there was no horse to be seen. They thought the noise might be associated with a recently deceased thoroughbred called Foxtrot who, on returning from working, had been in the habit of galloping round and round this field. On another occasion, one of their daughters was frightened by the sound of an invisible horse galloping around the field in the daytime. Things came to a head one day, when a number of horses in that top field were galloping madly round and round without stopping. Attributing this to being stirred up by the ghostly mare, Paul called out, 'Calm down, Foxtrot!' whereupon the galloping ceased, and there have been no more capers with her restless spirit since then.

PONSANOOTH (THE KENNALL VALE)

Those who are captivated by the haunting beauty of Kennall Vale, this oasis of tranquillity above Ponsanooth, may be surprised to learn how often that peace was shattered in the 19th century, recalling the old adage, 'In the midst of life, we are in death'. The rather paradoxical alliance of nature, engineering and science in this heavenly setting was highlighted by the *Cornish Telegraph* in 1887:

Kennall Vale itself, one of the loveliest spots in Cornwall, is very little known. It lies between Perranwell and Penryn and extends from Devoran to a little above Ponsanooth, a distance of about five miles. The most picturesque portion of the vale is in the possession of the Gunpowder Company and is, of course, rigorously closed to the public.

The road from Ponsanooth to the factory is extremely pretty, and before reaching the works, the magazine and the saltpetre refining house are seen on the right. Just inside the saltpetre house is the manager's house, beautifully situated, and a little beyond are the company's offices. These buildings extend practically across the valley, which at this point is narrow, and mark the point beyond which the public cannot go.

The ruined buildings of the old gunpowder mills retain an aura of past happenings.

The portion in the possession of the Gunpowder Company is about a mile in length, and it increases rapidly in steepness towards the head. Down the vale rushes a fine stream of water, and its power is utilised in driving all the machinery of the factory by means of water wheels, of which there are a large number.... Looking on the beauty of the machines and the singular peacefulness of the spot, it does seem incongruous that such a death-dealing agent should be manufactured there.

The waters of the pretty little river rising in the parish of Wendron were probably harnessed from early times, providing power for corn mills, paper mills, mining and allied industries over the centuries. Cornwall's first gunpowder factory was established in Cosawes Wood in 1809, which prompted the entrepreneurial Fox family, with widespread commercial interests in mining and shipping, to set up the Kennall Gunpowder Company in this idyllic setting. Gunpowder was in great demand for blasting in the mines and quarries, but this was a highly dangerous business and the industrial complex was designed to inhibit the spread of fire and break the force of explosions if accidents occurred. The floors were continually damped down, and more trees were planted to create a moister atmosphere.

Despite all the precautions, the local newspapers carried frequent reports of mishaps at the powder mills. A fatal accident in the mixing house in February 1826 was brought about by a female employee who had been roasting potatoes in another building some distance away and inadvertently transported a small spark in her clothing.

In January 1841, fate dealt a dreadful blow, when an early morning explosion in a mill where a large quantity of gunpowder was being stored, caused the only worker present to be decapitated. There was a harrowing account of his head being blown a considerable distance, with other parts of his body discovered in the branches of a tree. Several trees were uprooted by the blast, but the cause of the disaster was unknown.

Another blast, which blew a newly-erected stamping mill to atoms and rocked the Kennall Vale, occurred in January 1847. A contemporary newspaper stated: '*A number of persons, on hearing the report, congregated around the spot from the neighbouring village of Ponsanooth, and great was the lamentation among them, it not being known what family had been bereaved of its members.*' The mangled body parts of two men named Martin and Dunstan, which were found in the river and strewn across the area, created a shocking spectacle, and their remains had to be taken up in a large cloth.

A path through the once industrial Kennall Vale, where a ghostly figure lurks.

The brother of one of the victims had perished in the previous explosion at the factory. When the men were buried in Stithians' churchyard two days later, '*a vast concourse of deeply affected persons followed their remains to the grave*'.

One of the biggest bangs of all occurred shortly after the *Cornish Guardian's* description of the peace and beauty of the Kennall Vale in November 1887, when the folk of Camborne mistook it for gunfire from the fleet practising along the north coast. One man was killed and another was discovered badly injured in a leat. The cause of this disaster was thought to have been the result of friction created by dragging barrels of gunpowder across a dry floor, rather than being lifted bodily onto a cart.

By that time, the great depression in Cornish mining was leading to a slump in the demand for gunpowder, whose essential raw ingredients were charcoal, saltpetre and sulphur (brimstone). This was overtaken by advances in the development of the new nitroglycerine-based high explosives, such as dynamite and gelignite.

As the peace of the Kennall Vale returned, nature began to re-colonise the romantic industrial ruins, and it remains a haven for wildlife today.

It is not surprising that this scene of former intense industrial activity, where men in the prime of life met sudden and violent deaths, has also experienced some ghostly goings on. In recent years, various individuals have reported sightings of a ghostly figure lurking amid the ruins, who stares at them as they stare at him. He seems to be as curious about mortals as they are about spirits. Experienced ghost hunters who have had close encounters with phantom workers of old, have cited this as one of the places where time slips occur, comparable with a twisted film on a newsreel. One medium spoke of many presences and a general air of sadness.

Some walkers through the vale have described weird spatial experiences and distorted perceptions. One described the disconcerting sensation of walking backwards when his feet were going forwards, while the surrounding scenery became disproportionate and out of perspective. Sharp images with strange distortions and a certain floating quality, said to have been captured on film, remain a mystery to professional photographers.

ROCHE ROCK

Roche Rock, rising abruptly out of a wild and open expanse of rough and boggy moorland, dotted with old mine workings, is one of nature's wonders, which has always been a source of curiosity and awe. Alterations in the granite millions of years ago, making the surrounding softer kaolinised rock predisposed to erosion, left this tough, reef-like mass of tourmaline and quartz, known as schorl, as a bold and isolated feature in the landscape, which generations have sought to explain in myth and legend.

This dramatic and isolated rocky phenomenon, crowned by an ancient chapel, is steeped in mysticism.

This noble rock formation was of early sacred significance, and may itself have been an object of worship as well as being associated with a god or goddess. Tradition tells us that this was where a hermit chose to live a life of quiet contemplation, with his chapel above and a cell below. The striking granite-built chapel of St Michael, situated on the summit of the centre crag, was dedicated in 1409, and reputedly constructed by the last male heir of Tregarrick. It became the lonely refuge of a man stricken with leprosy, whose loving and dutiful daughter Gundred attended his daily needs until he died.

An 18th-century traveller who passed this way was struck by this strange place, describing it as 'a singular scene exhibiting a kind of wild sublimity, peculiar to itself'. This remains as true today as it ever was. The surrounding moors were the legendary hunting grounds of the heroic King Arthur, and the ruined chapel on Roche Rock is cited as the hermitage of Ogrin in the classical love story of Tristan and Yseult. These tragic lovers were not the only ones to seek refuge here, for the story goes that the infamous bogeyman John Tregeagle sought the sanctity of this elevated church while being pursued by the fiery eyed Hounds of Hell and got his head stuck in the east window in the process. Although he was freed, his unquiet spirit found no rest, and he returns to haunt the place when storm winds howl across the moors.

The impressive geological phenomenon comes as quite a shock to those who stumble upon it unexpectedly for the first time, generating feelings of fear, foreboding and general spookiness. There have been reports of a grim ghostly face peering out of a window of the ruined chapel when nobody was about, recalling the unfortunate leper who was incarcerated there for so long, and inexplicable eerie noises emanating from the vicinity. Ghostly shadows hurrying about among the rocks, bending over and fleeing upwards have been associated with miners from Great Beam Mine, which was being worked during the reign of Henry VIII, or Good Speed Mine, commonly known as Black Pepper Mine, where there were the inevitable mining accidents. Mention has also been made of a phantom monk, but cameras tend to 'play up' when attempts have been made to capture any of this on film.

Roche Rock has attracted the attention of various experts on the paranormal, who reckon the rock itself possesses a spirit and a personality. They see this as a predominantly peaceful, yet powerful place; a sacred, holy site.

ST DOMINICK (COTHELE HOUSE)

The ancient manor house of Cotehele, with its pleasing architecture and majestic wooded setting on the Tamar above Halton Quay, exudes an atmosphere of romantic antiquity. This estate came into the possession of the Edgcumbes, an old established Devon family, in 1353 when William Edgcumbe married Hilaria de Cotehele, and remained in their possession until being taken over by the National Trust in 1947. The Edgcumbes went on to

Cotehele, former home of the Edgcumbe family.

expand their estates and play a prominent political role in local life, but the colourful and heroic Sir Richard, who died in 1489, was the first member of the family to create an impact over a much wider area.

Sir Richard's exploits had produced a range of enemies, including his feuding neighbour Richard Willoughby, who attempted to ambush and murder him as he innocently rode home on one occasion, and burn down his house on another. Ironically, they subsequently became close friends, the families inter-married, and the Edgcumbes acquired their lands across the river.

When it came to rebuilding the manor house, Sir Richard incorporated features calculated to deter those who sought retribution, such as a restricted entrance, a battlemented tower and small windows.

The ruined chapel in the woods recalls the most famous of the legends surrounding Sir Richard. Having proclaimed his allegiance to the Earl of Richmond, later to become Henry VII, Sir Richard became an outlaw and took refuge at Cotehele. He was hunted down by Richard III's soldiers, led by Sir Henry Trenowth of Bodrugan. On hearing their approach, he cut the throat of a servant to avoid being betrayed and fled into the woods. With pursuers hot on his trail, he became trapped on an overhanging rock high above the river bank. In a moment of inspired desperation, he put a stone in his cap and cast it into the fast-flowing waters below. He then froze, hardly daring to breath. Hearing the splash and seeing the cap floating past, Bodrugan and his men assumed that their quarry had drowned and abandoned their search. Sir Richard, who was knighted at Bosworth, built a chapel here as an act of thanksgiving. He later died in France.

Sir Richard's son Piers, who was rewarded for bravery in battle, acquired more land, including the Edgcumbe estate overlooking Plymouth Sound, where his son Richard constructed a new house in 1553. This became the family's principal seat and they only made occasional visits to Cotehele, which was left in the care of a farmer and his wife.

After the death of the 3rd Earl, Ernest Augustus in 1861, his widow decided that she would like to end her days at Cotehele. Renovations were carried out in sympathetic style, with the east wing, formerly serving as a storage area with servants' quarters above, being transformed into a comfortable house for the dowager countess. After her death 20 years later, her rather straight-laced unmarried daughter, Lady Ernestine Edgcumbe, continued to live here until around 1905. The 5th Earl arrived at Cotehele in the early part of the Second World War, having been bombed out of Mount Edgcumbe. He died here in 1944.

The ultimate in spooky happenings, with a touch of poetic justice, is said to have occurred in 1742, when one of the proud Edgcumbe ladies was laid to rest in the domestic chapel at Cotehele. On the night after the funeral the knavish sexton had the audacity to creep down to the vault and force open the coffin. As he attempted to divest the lifeless fingers of their priceless rings, the 'corpse' began to stir and focus its eyes upon him. He let out a terrified scream, dropped everything and fled for his life. Whereupon the lady, who had been in a coma, emerged from the coffin and made her way up the dark stone steps by the light of the lantern the scoundrel had so obligingly left behind.

A number of strange happenings have been reported over the years, including sudden whiffs of a herbal-like fragrance in the east wing, where the dowager countess and her daughter had lived. One early National Trust assistant administrator felt this to be the ghostly presence of a lady who had been happy here, and was reluctant to leave. He would talk to it as it accompanied him around the house. Strains of plaintive music heard in the oldest part of the building might be linked with the 2nd Earl, who had a love of music and acting. A ghostly figure in old-fashioned dress seen in the vicinity of the archway leading to the present entrance of Cotehele, recalls the unfortunate servant whose throat was cut to prevent him giving information about Sir Richard's whereabouts. A stone with an apparently irremovable bloodstain, where the poor man had collapsed and bled to death, was painted over and repositioned some years before.

As the 5th Earl lay on his deathbed in the east wing during the Second World War, the local nurse in attendance noticed a woman in a long white dress enter the room and leave a few minutes later. Being a newcomer she took her to be the housekeeper, but when she came across that lady later in the day in a sober black uniform she made a remark about the white dress she had worn that morning. It transpired that the housekeeper knew nothing about a white dress and had not been in the sickroom. They came to the conclusion that it must have been a ghost, perhaps that of the Earl's wife who had died in 1935.

Finally, rather dramatically, it has been reported that a ghostly girl with long dark hair has been seen rushing down the stairs with arms raised. She is thought to be one of the domestic staff who fell to her death when pursuing the fleeing groom, who had apparently made her pregnant.

TRELISSICK

The majestic estuary of the Fal stretches northwards through the expansive area of Carrick Roads, with navigable creeks opening out on either side. Beyond Turnaware Bar, the waters narrow and flow between steeply-wooded shores, before dividing as the Fal and Truro rivers. These busy waterways, which had long been the principal means of trade and communication around these parts, became the haunt of pleasure seekers in the early days of tourism, with the river excursion between Falmouth and Truro being described as 'the most delightful in England' in one old guidebook.

There has long been a ferry crossing at the narrowest point of King Harry Reach, where tradition says that King Henry VI once braved the dark and treacherous waters on horseback. The ferry passage created an important link between the agricultural Roseland peninsula, and Truro and the mining area on the western side. Farmers used it for getting their stock across to Truro market.

At one time there were two ferry crossings; one by a rowed ferryboat for foot passengers from Tolverne to Kea, and the other a horseboat, which used this shorter crossing. Oared by two ferrymen aft, it was used to transport sheep, cattle and other livestock, as well as cargoes. When wind and weather made the going difficult, everybody would be called on to lend a hand.

It was quite a breakthrough when a new steam ferry came on the scene in 1889, and later a steam chain ferry, with the rather engaging appearance of a latter day Noah's ark. The design has continued to evolve to meet changing needs since then. At one time carriages and cars were carried athwart the transom (crossways), and loading and unloading with ramparts, blocks and planks could be a dicey business. Not surprisingly, the newspapers carried reports of horses, carriages and cars ending up in the river. This constricted, fast-flowing section of the river, which is deep and dangerous, has claimed many victims, and may well be the haunt of lost souls.

In view of all the dramatic events that have occurred here over the centuries, it may seem strange that the most powerful ghostly manifestation in this watery environment is associated with a child, rather than a waterman, and is centred on a quayside cottage, rather than the river. Mystery surrounds the supernatural activities which

King Harry Ferry and Quay Cottage, c.1880.

occur in Quay Cottage, adjacent to King Harry Ferry, where the Copeland family of Trelissick used to house their boatmen long before the estate was taken over by the National Trust.

Shortly after the head gardener Barry Champion moved into the cottage with his family, his young daughter, who occupied the smaller of two bedrooms above the lounge, came rushing into her parents' bedroom one night in a distressed state, saying that there was a young girl standing at the bottom of her bed. They comforted her and hauled her into bed, assuring her that there was nothing to be frightened about. However, she came into their

bedroom on a number of subsequent occasions saying, 'I've just seen someone walk through the wall', or 'Somebody's just walked through the closed door'. She said it was a little girl of about her own age, wearing a smock, as children did in the late 19th and early 20th century, who looked sad and pensive. It seems that the child and the phantom would regard each other with curiosity, until the phantom faded away.

Various occupants of this cottage at King Harry Ferry have spoken of a ghostly little girl.

The child's parents thought that there must be a rational explanation to all this, until the night that Linda Champion suddenly awoke feeling unaccountably cold. She sat up in bed and saw the figure of a girl aged about ten, standing in the doorway with one hand on the door jamb. She was peering into the bedroom. Linda shook her head in disbelief and the image vanished shortly afterwards. The manifestations continued in the daughter's bedroom and one Friday afternoon when Barry returned to the cottage for a cup of tea, he became aware of the sound of footsteps in the rooms above. Going upstairs to investigate, he found there was no one there. The same thing happened again and again and always on a Friday afternoon, with the footsteps always going from south to north. He thought this particularly odd, because weyrock (a type of hard-flooring) and thick carpeting covered the floorboards, which normally cushioned the sound of footsteps.

The Champion family had decided to keep this eerie information to themselves for fear of being ridiculed, until Linda was asked by a Mrs Coopper, whose family had had a close association with Quay Cottage, if they had encountered the ghost. According to some old timers, the daughter of a ferryman who once occupied the cottage, vanished without a trace and for some reason foul play was suspected. Barry and I mused about the child who haunted the two bedrooms and the significance of Friday afternoons.

With Barry's help I managed to track down Mrs Coopper, who had moved away to be nearer her family in old age. This bubbly lady recalled that her parents had started renting Quay Cottage from Mrs Ida Copeland shortly before the Second World War. They got an unexpected initiation soon afterwards when the bed they shared in the larger bedroom started banging violently up and down for no reason. They were understandably upset by this and somewhat baffled, and when it happened the place took on a very uneasy aura. Friends who came to stay and who occupied this bedroom had such a frightening experience on their first night that nothing would induce them to stay any longer. Young Mrs Coopper was sceptical about this until she went to visit, along with her husband, and also had a strange experience in that bedroom which smacked of the supernatural. It is thought that a man of the church was brought in to carry out an exorcism.

During her reminiscences Mrs Coopper also recalled that her parents mentioned a particularly unsavoury character who had tried to start a tearoom in the cottage some years previously. There was great concern about the cruel way he treated his young daughter and Mrs Coopper confided, 'My mother always said that she thought he'd murdered her and blocked her up in the wall'.

TRURO
(TRESILLIAN, KEA)

Truro, situated at the head of a navigable creek running northwards from the Fal estuary, was an important port long before Falmouth existed, and had the advantage of being tucked out of sight from seafaring marauders. The roads in Cornwall and the far west were notoriously bad and, for centuries, trade and communications had been primarily by water. Truro River was once busy with coastal and ocean-going vessels, and the area around the quaysides thronged with salty characters of all descriptions. It was a lively sort of environment, frequented by hard-drinking old sea dogs, where ships' masters and press gangs were on the look out for able-bodied young men to crew their vessels. It attracted prostitutes, pick pockets and a host of rogues and villains, and was a place where old scores were settled, where tempers flared and where knives were readily drawn. Numerous murders were committed here, with bodies being cast into the water.

Strange things have occurred around this wharfside area,
formerly the haunt of rollicking seafarers.

The brutal happenings in the days of yore have left a spooky legacy around the wharf-side area on both banks of the river. Strange happenings have been reported in the former warehouses, currently occupied by Blewett's Bakery and Radio Cornwall.

Hi-tech seems to merge with the supernatural at Radio Cornwall on Phoenix Wharf, where members of staff have long been convinced that the place is haunted. It is particularly eerie at night, with some people reluctant to go upstairs if the lights are off, and others refusing to do so at all. New staff or itinerant staff from London invariably say, 'Have you ever thought there is a presence in this building?' As broadcaster Duncan Warren put it, 'There is definitely something here. There is no doubt about that whatsoever!'

Truro had been on the rough and sometimes perilous old wagon routes into Cornwall, but fast and splendid stagecoaches came on the scene when the turnpike road was constructed, linking the packet port of Falmouth with London and other cities. In the late 18th and 19th centuries, when mining was booming, the streets of Truro were busy with horse-drawn buses and vans, forming regular links with the surrounding towns and villages. A number of inns and hostelries catered for the needs of local folk and visitors who converged here.

Successive landlords of the Wig and Pen have long been aware of a ghostly presence, with objects mysteriously moved around and feelings of not being alone. Stereos and taps which have been turned off somehow get turned on, and when some decorative naval plaques were put up around the area above the bar, they were repeatedly found stacked up on the bar the following morning, until the landlord politely requested the ghostly presence to let them be. On one occasion a member of the bar staff who had gone down to the cellar had carefully left the door open only to find herself trapped after it closed itself. Although it was not locked she was stuck in the cellar for an hour or so before the door finally gave way and she was released.

A former landlord who went down to the cellar around midnight got a feeling that he was not alone, before experiencing a sighting of a sad-eyed, fair-haired girl, apparently of another era, who gradually faded away after about 30 seconds. His colleagues wondered why his hair was standing on end when he returned to the bar. This sighting and other similar reports have been linked to Clare Jane Smith, who was knocked down in the road outside the pub by a horse carriage, in July 1885. The badly injured girl was brought into the pub, where she died soon afterwards, or as the present landlady put it, 'The poor girl was brought into the premises, and apparently she's stopped.'

Some months ago, when things were quiet in the bar and there were no females on the premises, a customer returned from the gents and informed the landlord that there was a young girl in there. The colour drained from his face and he made a hasty exit when it was explained to him that he had probably seen the resident ghost.

Truro had played a significant role in the religious life of the county long before the cathedral was built. A Dominican friary was established there in the 13th century and mention has been made of various ghostly friars. Staff working at the old city hospital, on a site purported to be that of a former nunnery, often had fleeting glimpses of nun-like figures reflected in shiny surfaces.

The site chosen for the new cathedral at High Cross in the late 19th century, had always been the focal point of everyday life in Truro. Staff working in the building on the corner, currently occupied by the Woolwich Building Society, are often aware of a presence there. Although it has quite a noisy position in the street, there are times when unexplained sounds seem to emanate from upstairs, as if some restless spirit were banging things about. Several people have felt a presence approaching from behind, when no one was there, and some address it in a friendly way. Various items have gone missing, never to re-appear.

A former member of staff got a shock the day she saw an apparently headless phantom come in through the door and evaporate a few seconds later. She subsequently discovered that hangings were once carried out at High Cross, and that there used to be a smithy at the adjacent Pearsons Ope. The story goes that the blacksmith was hanged here after wreaking terrible revenge when his sweetheart went off with another man.

There was a local tradition that Devil's Arch near Tresillian on the old route into Truro was haunted by a ruthless highwayman who was in the habit of dangling a noose from the parapet, with the intention of hanging the coach drivers and plundering the passengers' possessions in the ensuing chaos.

In 1810 it was reported that William Dunn, a travelling tailor was on his way home to Truro, when he saw a troop of little pixies (thought to house the spirits of the departed) ahead of him as he was passing Kea church. They were wearing identical red cloaks and black 'sugar loaf' hats, and he watched them run down the bank, cross the road in single file, and clamber over the hedge into the churchyard. They vanished when he rushed after them brandishing his stick.

·Bibliography·

Addicoat, Ian, *Ghostly Tales of Cornwall*, Akashic Books, 2001
Bottrell, William, *Cornish Ghosts & Legends*, Jarrold Publishing, 1981
Deane, Tony & Shaw, Tony, *The Folkore of Cornwall*
Dunn, Mike, *The Looe Island Story*, Polperro Heritage Press, 2005
Hole, Christine, *Haunted England*, Kessinger Publishing Co., 2004
Hunt, Robert, *Popular Romances of the West of England*, Ayer Co. Pub., 1968
Jenkin, A. J. Hamilton, *Cornwall and Its People*, David & Charles, 1973
Jenkin, A. J. Hamilton, *Mines and Miners of Cornwall*, Truro Bookshop, 1962
Mansell, Tony, *Mithian in the Parishes of St Agnes & Perranzabuloe*
Noall, Cyril, *Cornish Mine Disasters*, Truran, 1990
Norway, Arthur, *Highways & Byways in Cornwall*
Poole, Keith B., *Britain's Haunted Heritage*, Robert Hale Ltd., 1988
Rawe, Donald K., *Cornish Hauntings and Happenings*, Robert Hale Ltd., 1988
Salmon, Arthur, *The Heart of the West*
Smit, Tim, *The Lost Gardens of Heligan*, Orion, 2000
Turner, James, *Ghosts in the South West*, David & Charles, 1973
Underwood, Peter, *Ghosts of Cornwall*, Bossiney Books, 1998
Williams, Michael, *Hawker's Morwenstow*, Bossiney Books, 1988

The following were also consulted in the course of my research:

Fortean Times
Kelly's Directories
Old Cornwall magazines
Radio Cornwall
Cornish Studies Library, The Cornwall Centre, Redruth
Cornish Guardian
West Briton
Western Morning News
Cornish Telegraph, 1887
English Heritage
National Trust

•Index•